HOME INC.

The Business of Buying and Selling

a Luxury Home

Alex Goldstein and Brian Tracy

ISBN-13: 978-1492812739

ISBN-10: 1492812730

CONTENTS

———— ✳ ————

WARNING!

———— ✳ ————

This book does not pull any punches in revealing secrets that many industry insiders are unwilling to discuss. Here are just a few examples:

✳   Have you ever heard a real estate agent tell you that real estate agents are completely unnecessary? Well, Alex Goldstein says it right on page 6.

✳   When it comes to business, most conventional wisdom tells you to "follow your passion" and to "grind it out." Brian Tracy's expert advice flies right in the face of conventional wisdom, as he tells people to get out immediately if specific criteria are not met. Brian analyzes every financial and business decision through the lens of his powerful concept of Zero Based Thinking on page 88.

✳   The real estate industry has fundamentally changed, putting the client in the driver's seat and making greater demands on agent's skills than ever before. Yet many agents are living in the past, and still haven't adapted. You need to know how to separate the agents in your area who "get it" from those who don't. It's all revealed starting on page 22.

✳   Countless so-called gurus tell us that creativity is essential for finding the best solution to any type of a problem in business or life. But what if you're not creative? What do you do when that blank page is staring back at you? Brian Tracy explains the brilliant Mind Storming method for generating ideas in simple terms anyone can apply, starting on page 92.

The style of this book is conversational, based on interviews with the authors. We purposefully kept that format throughout the book, so that these important concepts remain accessible to a wider audience. The language is simple, but don't be fooled —the concepts are powerful, and are based on many years of experience and many proverbial battle scars.

The information in this book is useless if you don't apply it. Please take immediate action to benefit yourself and your family in real estate, business, and financial decisions. To help, we've made available to all of our readers, an Action Guide that provides step-by-step instructions to apply the techniques in this book. For this free resource, please visit: **www.HomeIncBook.com/SecretBonus**

We hope you enjoy reading this book as much as we've enjoyed writing it. Suggestions, comments, and questions are welcome, just visit: **www.HomeIncBook.com/Contact**

SECTION 1

THE BUSINESS OF REAL ESTATE

CHAPTER 1:

REAL ESTATE SECRETS

GREG

Welcome to this first module on the secrets most real estate industry insiders don't want you to know. My name is Greg Rollett, and today I am joined by real estate expert Alex Goldstein. Alex has over 11 years of experience in real estate throughout the state of Arizona. He is known for investing his clients' money with the same care he would show his own—a reputation which has earned him national recognition as a master negotiator for his clients.

His work and expertise have been documented in The New York Times, The Wall Street Journal and on Fox News among other major media outlets. An honors graduate of Northwestern University, Alex was also a visiting scholar at Oxford University. Prior to starting his real estate business, Alex was a bond trader for the world's largest insurance broker, and founded the ecommerce division of a print media company. As a wine expert, Alex has served on the boards of both the International Wine & Food Society and the Confrérie des Chevaliers du Tastevin.

Prior to representing clients as an agent, Alex was an investor and developer in over $50 million worth of transactions, and this experience on both sides of the table enables Alex to provide a level of service that is virtually unrivalled. His primary focus is on luxury real estate in Paradise Valley and Scottsdale, Arizona, and in addition to "traditional" luxury transactions Alex also has expertise in seller financing, auctions, and bank foreclosures.

GREG

Alex, welcome to today's program.

ALEX

Thanks for inviting me, Greg. It's great to be here.

GREG

Now, Alex, as we begin this first module, we're going to be talking about the secrets that most real estate industry insiders don't want you to know.

I want to begin by talking about some of the reasons that you got into real estate. Tell us what brought you here and explain what you're doing to change the way that buyers and sellers work with real estate agents.

ALEX

Thanks, Greg. I got into the business of real estate agency after spending years as an investor and developer. I started out on the side of the table where you write the big check, and after years of dealing with agents I started to see a gap in the marketplace. It became clear that clients deserved a better level of service than they were usually receiving.

It didn't seem to matter what area I was looking, the price point nor type of property, the experience wasn't meeting my expectations. This was especially problematic in Arizona because we have among the highest per capita rate of real estate agents in the United States.

So we have a lot of real estate agents, and it's hard to separate the wheat from the chaff. I got involved because I understood the situation from the client's perspective, and knew that I could deliver the kind of service that I wanted as a client. In a nutshell, that's how I got started—I wanted to provide a level of service that I couldn't find in the marketplace.

GREG

That's a great place to begin this program, seeing the transaction from the client's side. Let's look at the truth about real estate today and the way that many real estate agents work with their clients.

I want to start with something that might seem controversial to many in the real estate industry. It happens to be the biggest secret in real estate. Alex, why don't you shed some light on this eye-opening secret?

ALEX

The secret that's hiding in plain sight is that real estate agents are completely unnecessary. It may sound crazy for somebody who is a real estate agent to say that the whole profession isn't necessary, but the fact of the matter is that a real estate agent should only be involved in a transaction when they can add value to that transaction. There are many different types of transactions and many ways to add value, but agents have to be conscientious and diligent in their efforts.

The way I look at it: being a real estate agent is like being a chef. A restaurant is only successful if it makes and serves incredible food. If a restaurant delivers all of these things, then people go to the restaurant. But nobody ever *needs* to go to a restaurant. You can go to a grocery store, you can cook at home. Nobody has to go to a restaurant; everybody can cook for themselves.

The entire restaurant industry exists because it provides something that is either better or more convenient than what somebody can provide for themselves. If it didn't do that, the whole industry would cease to exist. It's exactly the same in real estate; it's just that most real estate agents don't recognize the simple fact that they're unnecessary. People can do this for themselves if they wanted to do so.

Of course, if the average person handles real estate transactions themselves, they are probably going to make mistakes due to their lack of experience, and those mistakes can be costly. Even if they do everything perfectly themselves, they will spend a lot of time managing the process. Thus, there are valid reasons to use the services of an expert real estate agent, but clients always have the choice to "walk out of the restaurant and cook at home"—my philosophy is it's best to acknowledge this rather than tap dance around the issue.

So the real secret is that the whole profession is unnecessary. As such, clients should demand a level of expertise and service that adds value. This is how I approach the service I provide for my clients: I am relentless in my efforts to improve my expertise and level of service, and I am grateful for the opportunity to work with wonderful clients.

It's critically important to not only maintain this service-focused mindset personally, but to ensure that each of my strategic partners has a similar attitude and commitment.

GREG

Alex, I appreciate you sharing that eye-opening reality. I have to ask, though, why do you believe we still hire real estate agents nearly every time we're going through a real estate transaction if they are truly unnecessary?

ALEX

First and foremost, real estate transactions are a huge decision. For many people it's the largest financial decision that they'll ever make. I don't think it's human nature to just "wing it" when there's a lot on the line. So there is a significant need for trained professionals committed to adding value for their clients.

The most important thing I can do for my clients is to help them make good decisions. As a real estate agent my role is not simply to provide information to my clients, but also to curate it—to help them understand what's meaningful and what's not from the huge amount of information available. The ability to effectively do this comes with experience.

I've negotiated millions of dollars worth of transactions, and developed systems to manage the processes. I also use technical and industry resources the average layperson wouldn't or couldn't utilize. My role is to bring all of this together to offer my clients a better experience. An agent should provide the client a much better experience than the client would have working on his or her own, saving them money and heartache.

The unfortunate reality is proven by awful statistics. I believe that it was Gannet that came out with a nationwide poll about how the American public perceives various professions; real estate agents weren't all that much better than Congress.

Because of my experience on the other side of the table, I understand why people are hesitant to get into a relationship with an agent. I know it's an uphill battle to try to convince cynics that I'm one of the good guys. So, I don't even try. Instead I focus on sharing great information and addressing their questions to the best of my ability. By doing this I know people will call me when the time is right, and if there's a mutual fit we'll work together.

GREG

You are clearly holding yourself to a high standard, but it sounds like the industry has a lot of problems. Why are you so committed to it?

ALEX

I love my profession and I love what I do. As the legendary business coach and consultant Dan Sullivan said, "All progress begins by telling the truth." We can't improve the industry unless we're honest about the things that aren't working.As a real estate professional I'm committed to dealing with the realities and challenges that face my industry.

Fundamentally, the problem starts with the fact that barriers to entry into the profession are low compared to other industries. The licensing requirements and costs associated with becoming a real estate agent are relatively small, and as a result we have a huge number of people working part-time within the profession. These people don't have much training or experience. They function at the legally mandated minimum level of competency, and that is low considering how much money is at stake. Real estate professionals must offer insightful, useful advice to their clients, guiding them through unfamiliar waters. This level of responsibility demands a high level of commitment and training.

The current system has harmed the reputation of the profession, and that's why I advocate that there be higher standards to which all agents should be held. If state authorities aren't going to hold agents to a higher standard, then the clients should do so. It's best for clients, agents, and the whole industry, and that is why I am outspoken on this subject.

GREG

I want to talk more deeply about the client and their needs. You've worked with many clients over the years. What have you learned from working with these clients?

ALEX

It can't be overstated how important it is to help clients make effective decisions. My background in real estate was as an investor, and I was a bond trader earlier in my career, so it's in my nature to think analytically. However, over time I've learned that buying a house is deeply, profoundly emotional—it's like getting married. Powerful emotions impact decision-making ability.

When people get married—even if it's a great decision for them to get married—it's not uncommon to get cold feet on the day of the wedding. Doubts come to the surface on the day of a big decision and it's common for people to question whether of a big decision and it's common for people to question whether they're doing the right thing.

It's in moments like this when folks want guidance; they put their trust in the people around them. Whether that comes in the form of a bride asking if she's making the right decision or a client having second thoughts about a house—their advisor carries a huge responsibility to listen and help guide them toward a good decision that they reach on their own. Nobody can make a decision for anyone else, they can only bring experience and empathy to the person who needs help.

In dealing with clients I've learned that even the most practical and sophisticated individual is susceptible to strong emotional swings during the buying process. As a real estate agent my job is to make the experience the best that it can be while helping them to make rational, thoughtful choices.

GREG

Alex, you said something to me once that I found shocking. You said "the client is not always right." This goes against everything I've ever heard. What do you mean?

ALEX

As Winston Churchill observed, "There are two reasons for everything—a good reason, and the real one." I'm going to go straight to the real one today.

Before I reveal what's behind the curtain, so to speak, I want to preface this by saying that I'm speaking about the industry in general. My clients are wonderful, of course; by the time they've become my client we've gotten to know each other well and there has been a meeting of the minds.

They may have spent months reading my materials, or we may have spent a lot of time speaking. Whatever the specific circumstances there's a connection and it's mutual. If not then we don't work together. My knowledge and experience are useless if I can't communicate with my client. If I've done my job before taking someone on as a client then we're working as a team. I want to be clear that I am grateful for my clients, and that my clients *are* right. After all they chose me, so they must be smart!

Kidding aside, here's the industry secret that's hiding in plain sight: clients are wrong when they don't demand expertise from their agents. Now you may think that's crazy, and that all clients demand expertise from their agents. However, that's not true and I can prove it. The most common example is awarding business to somebody simply because they're a member of the family or they have some other social connection. I'm all for working with family, but this is one of the most important financial decisions of your life.

Here's a recent example of how this decision can go wrong. A longtime newsletter subscriber called me to let me know that she was so impressed with the information and the analysis that I was providing her. She said she was convinced that I was the most qualified and committed agent, and the clear expert in the market and wanted to say thank you.

I was very flattered, of course, and I assured her that if we decided to work together that she would get the absolute best home-buying experience possible. Then there was an awkward pause in the conversation and she said, "Well, I'm dying to work with you…but I've been arguing with my husband. He's completely pigheaded and he absolutely insists upon my know-nothing brother-in-law representing us."

She went on a frustrated rant: "We want to buy a bank foreclosure and my brother-in-law has never done this type of transaction before. He doesn't even work in this area. It's totally stupid," she said, "I could scream." As she's telling me this I'm thinking to myself "This is the most significant decision of your life, and you are choosing to go with someone you know is unqualified." It blew me away.

To come back to the comparison I made earlier about eating in a restaurant, this is equivalent to dining at their brother-in-law's house and being served stale bread and burned meat. If they care about themselves they won't eat that food. They'll lovingly tell their brother-in-law that he's a lousy cook, tell him nothing, or fake a stomachache and then go out to eat.

It's amazing, but with something as insignificant as a meal people will be honest, or at the very least make a change. When it comes to this huge financial decision people lie to themselves. They make poor decisions that will affect them for the rest of their lives … all in order to be polite. There's nothing wrong with working with people with whom you have a great relationship, whether it's a social relationship or a family relationship—what's wrong is not doing your homework to make sure that the friend or family member advising and representing you is also qualified to do so.

What we see in a lot of cases are people who are not doing that. A lot of people are willing to hand over that decision to somebody that's not the most qualified person. This contributes to the problem that I've described—a problem that is pervasive in the profession—because it allows unqualified agents to hang-on. In other words clients are preventing unqualified agents from getting weeded out of the business by "doing them a favor." But wow, what a favor you're doing them risking millions of dollars with someone who is unqualified!

I understand that it can be difficult to say no to close friends or family, but there is so much at stake—both financially and personally. Not only will you have to live with this decision for a decade or more, but your doubts after the transaction is done can seriously harm the personal relationship you were trying to preserve in the first place. If you want to say no to awarding them the business, then do something really nice for them; buy them a bottle of wine or send them on a vacation, make them feel appreciated and they'll forget about the rest of it. It's certainly a lot cheaper than putting an unqualified person in charge of millions of dollars.

So that's what I mean when I say the client isn't always right. I work to ensure that I'm giving my clients everything they want, and I certainly want them to be right and want them to feel great about their decisions.

I provide information and analysis without any expectation

of being awarded the business, *even* to people who are working with their know-nothing brothers-in-law. I see it as my duty to serve the community and be the expert, regardless of compensation from any one person or transaction.

As the entertainment and fashion mogul Russell Simmons put it brilliantly: "Imagine if a comedian said, 'Sorry I can't be funny right now because nobody's paying me.' It's a comedian's job to be funny *all* of the time." So that's me, I'm a real estate guy *all* the time, not just when I'm getting paid.

GREG

Alex, that's a great statement about your commitment to the community. I really want to thank you for sharing that insight. It's helpful to identify with the issues facing clients, and you've pointed out some pitfalls that clients and agents alike should try to avoid.

At the core of the real estate industry is the fact that a real estate agent is a salesperson. When you're about to make the biggest financial decision of your life, you don't necessarily want to be working with a salesperson, someone who's traditionally pushy and someone that is trying to convince you to make a decision that you might not be ready to make. Let's talk more about a client's needs and mindset and what clients deserve from their real estate agent.

ALEX

Clients are looking for service and they're looking for guidance. It's the agent's job to fill these two key roles.

The agent's first job is to make sure that the clients are making the best possible decision. Agents must make sure that their client has the information to know if what they're contemplating is a sensible and prudent decision. That's a type of intellectual endeavor, and I provide information and analysis so that my clients can feel good that we've really looked at something thoroughly before making a decision.

The second part is the level of service agents provide. There are a lot of moving parts with a real estate transaction and ensuring that the process is straightforward for the client is crucial. From the first moment when somebody thinks, "I'd like to buy or sell a home," through closing a transaction, there are an awful lot of moving parts—documents, people and money. It helps to have someone experienced running the gauntlet on your behalf so that the client can focus on the outcome rather than the process.

With regard to real estate agents being salespeople—it's true that agents are usually compensated only upon the close of a transaction. However, that does not mean that real estate agents must be pushy. From my point of view there's more risk on the side of the agent in the beginning of the relationship than there is on the client side. After all, if I spend a lot of time with someone who isn't a good fit for my expertise and personality

I am never compensated for that. If I spent all of my time chasing after clients who weren't right, trying to put the square peg in the round hole so to speak, I would starve.

Some people are amazed that I turn down clients, but I am amazed more agents don't do this. Once I am committed to a client, I put in a lot of work, and am committed to putting it in as long as it takes until we find the right situation for the client—years of work is not uncommon. I am happy to do it, and it's part of being a professional, I would be nutty to try to work with everyone. Everyone isn't right for me, and I'm not right for everyone. So when I first speak to someone about a professional relationship, it's not pushy at all—it's an honest conversation to determine if there's a mutual fit.

GREG

It's very interesting that you take such a patient approach instead of the pushy approach that too many of us encounter too often. How do you maintain this patience when so many others take an opposite approach, don't you lose business?

ALEX

I view the profession that we should be experts in our market in order to provide value. I never pressure anybody into taking action because I believe that I'm the best at what I do, and trust that my investment of time and expertise into our relationship is never wasted. Even if nothing happens for years, I understand the value of delivering a great level of service and that when people are ready to act that investment will pay off.

My marketing focuses on information—sharing my expertise and letting people know about the service that's available to them: "Here's a free buyer's guide. Here's information on properties. Here's what you need to know if you're selling." I offer valuable resources that help educate people, and that's my way of starting the relationship. If people want more information and they have questions, then of course we can talk and see if there's a good fit.

The important point is to start relationships by offering information and giving advice without expectation of anything in return. I believe this approach establishes me as the preeminent expert, and I also believe that taking a long-term perspective establishes a client base that self-aggrandizing advertising and gimmicky sales pitches cannot. It pays not to rush—when the right deal comes along somebody's going to be working with me, and if it's not right for them we let it go and move on to the next thing.

For these reasons I am very, very adamant about not pressuring clients and making sure that everybody that comes to me knows that they'll never be under any pressure. I also make sure anybody that's associated with me will never pressure my clients and they are taking a long-term perspective rather than focusing on a short-term win. Patience may not be fashionable in this world of instant gratification, but it pays off. Warren

Buffett says it best: "No matter how great the talent or efforts, some things just take time. You can't produce a baby in one month by getting nine women pregnant."

I have more and better clients by being patient, so why would I ever be pushy? The *only* time it's appropriate to be pushy with a client is when time is of the essence, and they will lose money or a great opportunity by not taking action. In those situations I'm like white on rice making sure that everyone is moving the ball forward until it gets into the end zone.

GREG

Alex, this is really important for everyone to understand the difference between a salesperson and an expert advisor. In an earlier module, Brian Tracy spoke about a marketing approach that accomplishes the exact same thing that you're talking about.

By creating education and resources for clients, prospects and the general public, you're becoming the trusted expert that people can turn to, not just to be sold or pressured into a situation. There are a lot of people who don't grasp this concept, and it reminds me of real estate circa 1972.

ALEX

If you look at most markets, particularly in luxury segments, they're dominated by a handful of players. In many cases a lot of those folks have been in the marketplace for a very long time.

Obviously they have lots of relationships and they've done something right to be at the top of their game. However, I've also noticed that many of these individuals aren't keeping up with the times and they're taking—as you said—a 1972 approach. Such agents are (1) not making use of technology, and (2) selling rather than advising.

I am not somebody who uses technology for technology's sake; I use what's effective and what will help my clients. There is a lot of useful technology available and we can't live like we are still in an era dominated by fax machines. The impact of technology isn't as simple as the fact that anyone can go online and look at properties in a way that was unthinkable 10 years ago. Technology has changed the role of the agent in the process.

Daniel Pink wrote a wonderful book called *To Sell is Human* and one of his key points is that the difference between sales today and sales 25 years ago is that salespeople used to have a monopoly on information. That monopoly has evaporated, and the client is more informed than ever. This isn't just real estate, it's transformed every industry from cars to medicine— the client enters into the process with a great deal of information. Thus, to be relevant and add value, the agent has to provide meaningful analysis of this abundant information—curating overwhelming and sometimes misleading data in order to make the client's life better.

GREG

Why is it that there are still so many people who don't "get it"? Shouldn't the whole industry be aware of these changes affecting not only real estate, but the whole economy?

ALEX

Frankly, some in my profession aren't investing in their own training and skills beyond the legally required minimum. These agents usually fall into one of two camps.

The first group consists of agents who are at the bottom of the profession. It's the same as any other profession—you've got people who are lazy and they're never going to do more than the minimum. We can't help them, so they're not really worth discussion.

The second camp is noteworthy because it consists of individuals who are—or were—at the top of the profession, and are coasting on their reputations. It's important for clients to demand that they're with somebody who is continuously learning because the world is changing quickly.

Also, it's a lot more fun to work with someone who has a passion for what they're doing—someone who wants to be the best and that strives to get the best results.

I think about the wonderful film that came out last year called *Jiro Dreams of Sushi*. It's about a sushi master who was the first chef in Japan to be awarded three stars from the Michelin Guide. Jiro is revered as "the" ultimate sushi chef and he's in his 90s. He is thought of almost like a superhero in Japan amongst people who appreciate food, and even amongst competing chefs.

In this movie you see countless great testaments to his level of skill and mastery. Despite all of these accolades—this part gives me chills—Jiro says to the camera, "I have so much to learn."

It's profound to see somebody in his 90s who is undisputedly the number one person in his profession and to discover that his attitude toward his level of expertise is: "I have so much to learn." It speaks to the mindset that is required of this level of excellence and I try to model that behavior. I hope that no matter what success I enjoy, I'll always have that desire and motivation to learn.

GREG

Alex, I really appreciate you sharing that. This begs the million-dollar question: how do we find an agent that truly gets it?

ALEX

A great analogy is dating. If you're on a first date and all the person does is talk about themselves, there won't be a second date will there? However, if they are focused on you, that's a much more promising start to a courtship.

It's important to pay attention to the entire process, and it starts with the advertisements, because any professional is going to be—and this is not just real estate, this is any industry—trying to generate new business, that's the lifeblood of sustaining any business. We all have to do some kind of outreach to our community to bring people in the door.

My advice is to look at what those people are doing to attract your attention and how they want to start the relationship with you. When you look at an advertisement, ask yourself very simply: is that advertisement oriented to *me*, the client, and delivering something of value—or is it oriented to *them*, the agent, and promoting their name and smiling face?

This is a very telling thing, because you know how the rest of the relationship is going to go on the basis of that. If when they're trying to woo you their mind is focused on themselves, you can only imagine after you may have signed on as a client how that mentality may persist. It's something that is pretty easy to spot, you just have to know to look for it.

I am willing to bet that in any market where there are a lot of agents serving, you're going to find at least one person who cares about being the expert and educating clients. They should be willing to give all kinds of information and analysis, and to help without an expectation of some immediate gratification. So if you see that represented in the first communication with you, then that's a good indication their attitude is solid. That approach should carry over into a working relationship.

GREG

Alex, I really appreciate you breaking down how we can really find that agent. I want to take this discussion to the next level: how do you develop rapport or a relationship with an agent that can help you find the home of your dreams?

ALEX

It's important to invest some time with the agent that you're considering. If you're in a rush, then you just have to make the best quick decision that you can—their marketing and the quality of the information that they provide to you speaks volumes about the experience that you'll have.

However, most people are not making this decision quickly. Usually, they're going to spend some time getting oriented with the market and getting to know people before they start seriously considering a transaction. Having a long runway, so to speak, and allowing yourself time to watch the individual that you're considering is a great advantage.

For example, when somebody starts communicating with me, I'm going to provide them information for a very long time, for years and years if they want it. I don't simply say, "Here's a bunch of reports," and that's the end of the communication I have with potential clients. I've got a newsletter that is the preeminent newsletter in my market, describing everything that's happening so that people are fully informed.

This provides them with the opportunity to get my assessment of the market and to get the facts. My newsletter recipients receive all sorts of information that they can't get anywhere else, and I offer this at no cost. This continues for as long as they find it helpful.

I've had subscribers for years, including other professionals in my market like accountants and attorneys who may not even live in my area. Many of these professionals have clients in the area and they want to do right by their clients, so they read my newsletter to be kept apprised of what's going on in the marketplace. I'm here to serve the community, regardless of whether any one person will become a client.

I encourage people considering a real estate agent to evaluate what the agent provides up-front, and then to evaluate what this individual continues to provide. First impressions are important and you'll be best served in the long-run by someone that consistently offers information and service for the duration of your relationship.

GREG

That's great insight, Alex. Just like in business, this really is a relationship game and finding that right real estate agent is about building an enduring, mutually beneficial relationship.

As we begin to wrap up this first module, what I'd love to do is give everyone some first steps to take in their own situation. If we're in that stage where we're getting ready to make this biggest financial decision of our lives, what steps should we take to find the right agent and to put ourselves in a position to get what we want?

ALEX

The easiest thing for somebody to do is to start searching online, because clearly there will be a lot of people that are offering information. Start requesting information to evaluate what agents provide.

Are you getting something really substantial from them, and are they really an expert in their market? Are they really keeping pace? Are they somebody who's providing fresh and valuable information on a consistent basis? If you reach out to a group of real estate agents in your area and evaluate the information and correspondence that comes to you over the course of 30 days, it should be pretty clear who is walking the walk versus just talking the talk.

GREG

Alex, again, I think that's a great first step for everyone to take. Get started by searching online, look at agents' websites and blogs, and see the information that they are providing for you and see if they can become a trusted expert or advisor to help you through this process.

Clients should find an expert providing value to the community. In the Action Guide there is space where readers can map out some of this information to help them evaluate real estate agents in their areas.

In the next module we'll cover how you can negotiate the best deal for your home, one of the most important processes during the real estate transaction.

SUMMARY

YOU DON'T NEED AN AGENT

Agents should be involved in real estate transactions only when they add value. Don't hire an agent unless they demonstrate expertise and service. Demonstrate is the key word – anyone can say they are an expert, but the person who demonstrates it day after day, and week after week, is an expert.

IF YOU MUST USE AN AGENT, GET THE RIGHT ONE

Ask yourself when evaluating an agent: are they trying to advise you or sell you? Are their advertisements focused on themselves, or do they offer valuable information? What resources are they providing that demonstrate their expertise, and that help you become better informed?

TREAT BUYING OR SELLING A HOME LIKE A BUSINESS

Buying or selling a home is one of the most significant financial decisions in a person's lifetime. Invest time in finding professionals with expertise, from the agent to the attorney and everyone in between.

GO BEYOND YOUR SOCIAL CIRCLE

Virtually everyone has a real estate agent in their social circle or family, and odds are they are nice and well-meaning people. However, are they really the most qualified for the job?

This is a major financial decision you may have to live with for a very long time. It could have a substantial negative impact on that personal relationship.

Top Dogs Can Be Lazy

There may be a real estate agent with more signs in town than anyone else, but they may not give you much attention. They're also playing a numbers game, and they can be blasé about the outcome of any given transaction. Get the expert in your market who will focus on you, and who has a real passion for their work.

Never Feel Pressured

A serious professional will never pressure you to make a decision, and will provide advice and service long before a transaction may ever be involved. If you feel pressured by a real estate agent, it's the wrong agent.

CHAPTER 2:

EFFECTIVE NEGOTIATING
TECHNIQUES FOR REAL ESTATE

GREG

This second module will focus on negotiating the best deal for your home. My name is Greg Rollett and once again I'm joined by real estate expert Alex Goldstein.

Alex, before we dig into the how, I want you to give us an overview. Why is negotiation such an important step in treating the purchase of your home just like you would a business?

ALEX

Buying a home is just like any other major financial decision. You want to get the best deal. There is an old proverb that "bought right is half sold", and there's a good deal of truth to that. You want to get the best deal possible, but it's also a home and there's emotion involved in the decision as well.

There's a lot of negotiation in the process of buying or selling a home, and this is where experience begins to pay tremendous dividends, because it allows you to balance the importance of your investment with the emotional and personal facets of creating a home for yourself and your family. Navigating that maze can be very challenging, and that's where being with someone who has negotiated many, many millions of dollars worth of transactions really pays off. Balancing the emotional and financial sides of this transaction is a valuable role filled by a trusted advisor.

GREG

Alex, I want to go back a little bit into your story because you're actually a Master Certified Negotiation Expert. I want to talk a little bit about, one, what does that mean, and two, what does someone with that kind of experience bring to the table to help us get the best deal possible?

ALEX

The Master Certified Negotiation Expert is a credential that I was awarded. At the time I was awarded it there were only 220 people who had ever received it, as opposed to the basic level Certified Negotiation Expert, of which there are about 15,000. So it's an elite designation and I was honored to be recognized.

The reason that I invested the energy and time to get this credential was because I wanted to get some additional academic background to complement my real-world experience. Like Jiro, the great Japanese sushi chef I mentioned earlier, I always want to be learning and improving.

GREG

Given your years of experience successfully negotiating real estate deals both as an investor and an agent, can you explain how negotiations work for parties on both sides of the table?

ALEX

My primary job is to help people make effective decisions.

An effective negotiation starts with making an effective decision. Before you even begin to negotiate, you start with what negotiating professionals call the BATNA.

BATNA is an acronym for the Best Alternative To Negotiated Agreement. What that means is before you even sit down to the negotiating table, you want to define what happens if you can't reach an acceptable agreement. What's your next alternative? In other words, what is your Plan B? While this may sound obvious, it's something that most people don't think about, let alone write on paper. The problem with not having a BATNA before you start your negotiation is that when you're in the heat of battle, so to speak, your emotions take charge.

So if you don't have anything to lean back on, to know what you were thinking before you got into the negotiation, you can be flimsy or impulsive. This isn't to say that the BATNA is written in stone, it's a starting point. It's sensible to have a rational Plan B on paper, so you can look back and say, "When I was dispassionate, this is what I thought was the best alternative to a negotiated agreement." That's where we start before we even get into the negotiation.

From there, a critical part of the process of negotiation is being prepared and having reviewed a lot of information. This allows you to understand the relative strength and weakness of both parties.

Some of this comes from the statistical information that we can gather about what's going on in the marketplace and looking at that deeply and carefully. Then there's also human intelligence, where you are trying to gather information about what is happening in the life of the person on the other side of the table. The goal there is to get some sense of what might motivate them to act in a way that isn't necessarily something you can understand by looking at the numbers. We're all thinking, feeling beings, and we all make decisions that aren't necessarily 100% rational.

If you can gain some insight into what might be happening on the other side of the table, that offers you an advantage during negotiations. Combine that with a thoughtfully defined statement about your own desires and the strength and weakness of your position and you create a favorable negotiating position before offers begin to go back and forth. These are all things that I do before the first offer is going out the door to ensure a successful negotiation for my clients.

GREG

Alex, it's really crucial to understand the negotiation process that you just broke down. Something that I want to talk about is as you see these negotiations proceed, what's the number one thing that you see buyers do that absolutely ruins their chance of success?

ALEX

The worst thing that anybody can do in a negotiation is to negotiate for themselves. This doesn't just apply to real estate negotiations—it applies to anything where emotion is involved. We're our own worst enemy during negotiations where we are emotionally invested in the outcome, and this obscures our goals and limits our ability to make rational decisions.

There's a great negotiator named Herb Cohen who's written many books, negotiated during hostage crises and for Presidents and all sorts of incredible things, just an amazing man. His motto is, "In a negotiation, you want to care... *but not that much.*" As he says, the problem is that when you're negotiating for yourself, it's the 'not that much' part that is virtually impossible.

Herb has some hilarious stories of failed negotiations for himself because his emotions ran amok. Even this legendary man who has literally had lives on the line in negotiations admits that he is lousy at negotiating for himself when something is important and he cares too much about the outcome.

This is why I feel that people shouldn't negotiate on their behalf in an emotionally charged situation—particularly when it's a very important decision like purchasing a home. Not only is it an important financial decision, but if you've got a family you're talking about things that are going to impact the quality of your family's life.

If you've got somebody who's an expert whom you trust running the negotiation for you—do yourself a favor and *let them run it for you.* Obviously it's their job to get you as much as they can, but at the end of the day it comes down to, well, if we can't quite hit that mark that we were hoping for, would it be a good decision to take what we can get, or would it make more sense to walk away and live to fight another day?

That is where you should be relying on your expert, because it's too easy to be in the heat of battle and to make a decision that isn't necessarily a smart long-term decision. This is where I add a huge amount of value for my clients, because while I care about their interests I can still be dispassionate and bring information, tools and experience to bear on negotiations— making the outcome as good as it can possibly be.

GREG

Alex, this just reiterates a lot of what we covered in the previous module about finding that trusted advisor to help you during the transaction process and in that negotiation process. Let's start talking more specifically about the things that happen during the negotiation process.

You say that there are some very important questions that we need to ask before the actual negotiation begins. I was hoping you could share those questions with us, and explain why these questions are important to ask *before* we get stuck into a situation.

ALEX

I've said this before, and given its importance I'll risk beating a dead horse: it all starts with what is our Best Alternative To Negotiated Agreement? That's one of the most important questions we can ask. If we don't know what happens when we walk away from the table, we may stay at the table too long or leave too quickly.

Another important question to ask is, "Who has the greater time constraint?" As you get into a negotiation, people are always focused on the dollars. "Okay, I want X. X is my number, don't talk to me unless you get me X," and that's the mentality that a lot of people have when they go into a negotiation. However, there are a lot of other dimensions to negotiation, and the dimension that may in some cases be more powerful than money is time, and I don't think enough people give serious consideration to time.

So if you're a buyer you have to ask yourself: do you have the luxury of taking a lot of time to buy a home? Are you under any kind of time constraint? Conversely, as a seller, do you have a time constraint? Is there something that would be pressuring you to make a move? It's not just your personal situation, you also want to take into account the market—if market conditions are changing rapidly then time becomes more important for either the buyer or seller, depending on which direction things are moving.

Another question that is valuable to ask: are there other non-monetary considerations on either side that may be significant? This is a very open-ended question and it's important to think broadly about what, besides money, may be important to people. You want to ask that of yourselves, and you also want to ask it on the other side of the table. If the two sides are really far apart on their numbers, it is sometimes possible to bring these non-monetary considerations into play as a means to meet in the middle.

These are all questions that I like to ask when we get started, and there are a lot more of them I'll ask over time. I have a whole process, and that is at the heart of the matter: treat negotiation as a process, so there is a method to the madness, so to speak. It's not about winging it or trying to be a silver-tongued devil to get somebody on the other side of the table to do something that they don't want to do.

I'm going to gather as much information as possible, and then I'm going to leverage that information to get the best possible outcome. I can't guarantee a result of X or Y at any given time, but what I can say is I'd much rather go into a negotiation fully prepared with a well thought-out strategy.

Settling on your client's ideal number may make your client happy, however you may be doing that client a disservice. Maybe the client could get a better number and they don't even know it. Even if it makes my job as an agent and as a negotiator more difficult, I still want to raise that issue and say, "Hey, you know what? I think you might be letting them off the hook too easy," and we try harder.

In closing, I want to reiterate the importance of having a process in place. Don't wing it during important negotiations and leave the outcome to chance. Your family's home is too important.

GREG

This is very thorough, thank you. However, I wonder if we always have to be so methodical in the negotiation process, or are there exceptions or reasons why we might not want to do all of this?

ALEX

Good point, and it's worth noting that negotiations are not always lengthy or complex. If the market is moving fast or the deal on the table is exceptional, then the smart thing is to not overthink or delay. Especially as a buyer this is the case because you have an inspection period so if you've been too hasty you can usually walk away without penalty—but if you've been too slow, well then you've missed the deal. So, in a fast market "shoot first and ask questions later" is often the best way to proceed.

In 2013, it's a seller's market across the board. However, the higher one goes in price, the more challenging valuation becomes, and the more useful this structured negotiation process becomes. In other words, even in a strong seller's market, at the high end of luxury homes there's still sufficient time to be methodical in negotiations.

GREG

Alex, that was such a great breakdown and those questions that you need to ask yourself are in your Action Guide for you to implement when you're working with your real estate agent during this transaction process.

What we're going to do now is to talk a little bit about that process to help you to prepare yourself to win. Alex, let's talk about your process and your system that everyone going through this program can use in negotiations.

ALEX

We've talked about a lot of the key elements of preparation, and as you proceed you want to remember to ask open-ended questions. If you're a buyer, the obvious questions to ask of a seller are "Why are you moving?" and "Where are you going?" Open-ended questions often procure information that gives you an insight into their psychology.

I also encourage people to ask questions repeatedly, and to not just take the first answer that they hear. For instance, you may have an occasion to meet a seller as well as an agent, and so there's no reason that you couldn't ask the same question twice. Or there may be co-listed agents, so you have multiple agents who may reveal different things. Similarly on the buyer side there may be multiple buyers, as well as family members who have strong influence, so why not get all these different perspectives? Asking open-ended questions and quietly and listening can be a really powerful tool, and it's something that people aren't usually doing to the extent they could be.

That's what you do in the information-gathering phase. Then, when you begin to put together an offer, you want to revisit your BATNA and talk about where you were when you started and then look at that again once you've gathered information. At this point ask yourself: "Okay, do we still believe that the best alternative to negotiation is X?"

In most cases if you're looking to buy a house, basically your options are if you don't buy this house you're either going to buy another house or maybe there's no other suitable house that will become available and you'll have to wait on the market. Ask yourself: "If there are no other homes I like and I'm waiting on the market is the market rising? Is waiting going to cost me a lot of money?" Thinking through these consequences is key and provides context to your decisions and direction for your negotiation process.

Conversely, if you're a seller, you think through the future possibilities in a similar fashion. If you're looking to sell and you don't take this offer, what happens next? Well, then you wait for another offer. Next you think through what follows: "What do I really think is likely to come down the pike and when is that going to happen? What are my carrying costs?" This allows you to evaluate your next offer and think practically about what it needs to be in order to be better than what's currently on the table?

You want to continually revisit your circumstances and make sure that as you get more information that you're coming back to re-evaluate your opinions, ensuring that your assumptions are still valid. Then when it comes to putting together the offer, I believe it's important to be very clear and simple with language.

There are a lot of people that like to make their documents extremely elaborate to cover lots of different circumstances. I'm not an attorney, and my perspective on this is that you want to make it easy for the other party to understand your offer, because if they don't understand it then they're certainly not going to want to accept it.

While this sounds obvious, I see a number of people that try to deal with every possible contingency in their contracts. In my experience when you make your offer too complicated, even if it's fundamentally a good deal for both sides, you scare the person on the other side of the table.

In Arizona, we have an inspection period and there are a lot of documents that are drafted in escrow. It seems to me *that* is the point in time you should start dotting the i's and crossing the t's. If you make the main points of the deal easy to understand, you have a better chance of having it accepted. If you try to frontload all of these contingencies, then you're making the offer hard to understand and therefore hard to accept. So those are some of the specifics in terms of questions to ask and how to craft language.

Before you submit the offer, what you want to try to do as well is come up with some kind of a guess as to whether you believe it's possible to conclude the negotiations quickly, or if you're likely to have an extended round of negotiations. Sometimes you are just flying blind and you can't ascertain this. However, it's worth trying to ascertain this information—asking that question and putting this in your process. If you expect that you're going to have multiple rounds of negotiation, then you're going to want to structure your offer differently than if you think you're going to get one bite at the apple and that's that.

So those are some of the key points in the process. Of course there's even more involved as we sit down to do it and there are things that are specific to certain types of properties and so forth, but I think that the points just covered are superb tools to start navigating most negotiations.

These negotiating tools and this process may seem obvious, however the truth is that most people in most negotiations aren't taking this powerful approach. They aren't taking the time to prepare.

GREG

Alex, that's enlightening. Something that you've talked about that we need to touch on today is patience, because you say as we rush things we don't get optimal results.

This is really similar to a business jumping to conclusions or making assumptions about their customers or their marketing. I was hoping you could talk to us about what being in a rush can do to negatively impact our negotiations.

ALEX

This comes back to the discussion we had earlier about asking who has time and who doesn't. One of the most tried-and-true proverbs of negotiation is "He who is in a rush loses." If you must take action, you lose a lot of leverage, and you get desperate.

It's like dating; the guy who walks into the bar and feels like he has to meet a girl that night comes off as desperate and it never works. If you want to meet somebody and connect with them you can't be desperate. You should be interested and interesting, but you can't be desperate.

Being in a rush makes you desperate, and it clouds your judgment. It also is a very clear signal to anyone who's astute on the opposite side of the table that you're under constraints. This knocks the wind out of your sails and offers them the upper hand.

However, there are some times when you are in a rush and you have to be, and in those cases it's important to be realistic about what you can accomplish in a negotiation. If you simply must take action and it's very clear to the other side that you've got to take action, then don't delude yourself into thinking that you're also going to get the best possible terms. Do your best to neutralize the constraints, and to keep from giving away key information.

These are all things to keep in mind, and in a perfect negotiation if you really want to have the optimal outcome, the best thing you can do is to not be in a rush. The second-best thing is if you are in a rush, you want to make sure that you don't *appear* to be in a rush. So as long as you don't have that appearance, then hopefully you can protect yourself against any of the negative consequences that come with it.

GREG

That makes a lot of sense, Alex.

As Brian Tracy explained in his materials, we can learn a lot from going back to some old ways that produce some exceptional results. In the negotiation process this is true as well, so can you share some of these old, forgotten negotiation strategies with us?

ALEX

Some of the things that we've talked about really are tried and true. You want to ask a lot of questions, you want to gather a lot of information, you don't want to be in a rush; these are all key elements of successful negotiation.

You also want to try to get to know the person on the other side of the table as well as possible. There are situations where a human touch can be the thing that gets the deal done, particularly when you're in a really competitive environment.

There are certain segments of the market where the demand for property is so great that a bank foreclosure can receive over 50 offers within 24 hours. It's completely overwhelming for the person on the receiving end. That's a situation where having a relationship with the person who is reviewing those offers can go a long way.

Of course 50 offers is an extreme case, so to come to something more common in a traditional sale: if you're the buyer, get to know what the seller is doing. Conversely, if you're a seller, get to know what the buyer wants, because you may be able to bring some of those non-monetary considerations into the picture.

Someone who's selling wants their home to go to someone who's going to value it the way they do. That means something to people. They don't want to think of the place that they raised their children as just some box. It means a lot to them; it's got an emotional significance. Somebody who's buying a home is not just buying a box; they're buying the place they're going to make their home. It's emotionally powerful on both sides of the table.

To the extent that you can create a bond and get to know somebody, you may be able to bring some things to the table that make a person feel good about accepting a deal that they wouldn't necessarily take just on a by-the-numbers basis.

That's not to say that a handshake and "warm and fuzzies" are going to get you a million dollars off a property, but it could be the difference between getting close enough to get a deal done or to get some terms changed, versus not being able to get them.

I always encourage people to invest the time and energy in that human bond when things are getting contentious or even better, to prevent things from getting contentious in the first place. Reiterating what Brian Tracy is talking about—it comes down to sales.

You want to do more than present an offer by sliding a piece of paper across the table; you want to sell it, and you want to sell it to everybody who's involved, and that means getting to know people, whether it's the agent on the other side of the deal or whether it's the seller themselves or the buyer.

Get to know people and don't just make it about numbers; try to create some human bond and make a sale. Do some good old-fashioned work, talk to people, bond with them and do some selling. I think that's exactly what Brian Tracy would counsel as well.

GREG

Alex, I couldn't agree more. Really, that is sage advice to recycle some of these old, forgotten ways because they're still effective. Sometimes we get so distracted by shiny tools and the new gadget of the week that using some of these old negotiation strategies and sales strategies can help the negotiation process.

As we wrap up here in this second module, I'd love it if you could give some specific action steps for those going through this program to effectively plan to get through the negotiation process and broker the deal that's going to deliver them their new home. What can we do right now as soon as this interview ends to get the best result during negotiations?

ALEX

The first thing is start with the BATNA, the Best Alternative to Negotiated Agreement. Write it down; it's not enough to just talk about it. You've got to write it down on a piece of paper and say to yourself, "Okay, so if I don't buy this home or if I don't sell this home, if this doesn't happen in this negotiation, what do I do next? What's the next best thing that could happen for me?"

Write that down on paper so that you're giving clear thought to what happens next. Again, it's not written in stone and you may want to change it over time, but at least you've got something in writing that gives you the starting point.

The way the Harvard Negotiation Project defines a successful negotiation is if both sides achieve an outcome that is better than their BATNA. That's a successful outcome because, by definition, that means that everybody got something more than they would have gotten by not negotiating.

That's the academic framework for thinking about this, and everything else from there on is really where the rubber meets the road. You get away from the academic stuff and you start being an investigator.

Put on your detective hat, play Columbo, play Sherlock Holmes, get as much information as you can from the people that are associated with the transaction. Utilize your agent's expertise in statistical analysis and listen to his or her interpretation of the numbers. What were the other properties that are either on-market or closed? How were they different from the property that's currently on-market? How long did they take to sell? Your agent should really dig in and not just throw out a bunch of numbers at you. It's their job to help you make sense of those numbers and say, "Okay, what's significant and what's not? What's relevant and what's not?" This way you'll have a great deal of useful information and context to use during negotiation.

Once you've got that done, look back at your BATNA and think about some of the other questions that we've asked in terms of your timeframe and other non-monetary constraints;

make sure that you're comfortable, that what you want to accomplish is in sync with your best alternative to negotiation. That's when you start putting pen to paper and coming up with a strategy for negotiation and say, "Okay, this is the result that we would like to get, this is the result that we can live with, and this is the result would have us tap dancing on the ceiling."

When you have these things written down on paper, it prevents you from making a dumb decision in the heat of the moment.

GREG

Alex, you've mentioned in the past that there is a sure fire way to guarantee failure in negotiation. What is this and how can we avoid it?

ALEX

The number-one way to guarantee that you mess up the negotiation is to look a gift horse in the mouth. It happens sometimes that people will make a decision about what they want to get from a negotiation, and when they get it, they then decide that they want more.

The value of having your goals written down is you can refer back to them. If you came up with a set of terms that you thought would be shooting for the moon and you actually got them—accept them! Don't get greedy.

Don't decide that now you want the sun, the moon, *and* the stars—something bad always seems to happen once people think that way. I've seen it before, where somebody will literally get the best outcome that they could have imagined, and then they'll start to question it and they'll start to want to get the last nickel and so forth.

There's a real danger there because that can go on forever and you can wind up in a situation where you're never, ever happy with any outcome. You can mess up your negotiation, guaranteed, by not writing down any of this information and by allowing yourself to get so caught up in the negotiations that you get greedy and mess up a phenomenal deal.

Just because it's on the table now doesn't mean it's going to be on the table forever, so when you do get that gift horse, run with it. Don't question it.

GREG

Alex, that is such a great place to wrap up this second module. Again, start with the BATNA and know the end results that you want from the negotiation process. Go through all the questions and the resources that Alex has laid out for you in order to effectively go through your negotiation to find the best deal for your home.

Go through that Action Guide, go through those resources, and put them into play. In the next module Alex is going to be breaking down the process from the contract to the closing, and everyone and everything that is involved with getting you into your new home.

SUMMARY

ESTABLISH YOUR BATNA

What is the Best Alternative to Negotiated Agreement? Write it down so you don't make a poor decision in the heat of negotiations, and also to ensure everyone involved in the negotiation is working toward the same goal.

ASK OPEN ENDED QUESTIONS

If you're the buyer, ask the seller questions like "Why are you moving?" or "How soon do you think you could be moved out?" These questions will frequently yield insights that you can use to your advantage.

ASK QUESTIONS REPEATEDLY

Don't just accept the first answer you hear. Use every meeting with the person on the opposite side of the negotiation—and their agents, associates, or family—to your advantage.

RECONSIDER YOUR BATNA

Once you've gathered information, reconsider your options. Do you still think you have a good alternative to negotiation? What are the consequences if you don't reach a negotiation? Revisit these things to ensure that your assumptions are still valid, and whether your negotiating position should change.

TIME MAY BE MORE IMPORTANT THAN MONEY

Do you suspect that you will go through multiple rounds of negotiation or that you will present an offer and get an immediate response? Try to predict the process so you can know how to approach the first offer you will submit. Also, make sure you investigate any time constraints that the other side may have, this could lead to huge concessions.

MAKE YOUR OFFER CLEAR AND SIMPLE

Make the main points of the deal easy to understand so you have a better chance of actually getting it accepted. Outlining every contingency or using uncommon language can confuse the other side and potentially lose the deal.

CHAPTER 3:

CLOSING THE DEAL AND

PROTECTING YOUR ASSETS LONG TERM

GREG

Hi, and welcome back to this third module on "From the Contract to the Closing." My name is Greg Rollett and once again I am joined by real estate expert Alex Goldstein. Here in this third module we're going to be walking through the final stages of your real estate transaction.

Alex, I want to begin by talking about "the cast of thousands at a cost of millions" you've mentioned in the past.

ALEX

I used to be a bond trader for Aon Corporation, and the Chief Investment Officer of the company used to say that to me when we'd review proposals. He'd look at a big project and say, "It's a cast of thousands at a cost of millions," and it usually got a laugh. That is a perfect way to summarize what happens to get a real estate deal from contract to closing. There are so many different people that are involved that put their hands on this, and the amount of money at stake can be very substantial.

I want to briefly overview of all the people involved, and talk about the right way make it come together without driving yourself crazy.

Foremost, there's the agent, and their role in this process is to be the glue, to make sure that everybody's in touch with everybody else, and that all the pieces of the puzzle fit together...

and there are a *lot* of pieces to the puzzle.

Harkening back to our earlier discussion, this is another area where having an experienced agent to quarterback the process is a huge benefit. It saves an enormous amount of aggravation and can prevent a lot of problems. A good agent adds tremendous value in this part of the process.

Another key person in this process is the escrow officer. For those who may have never been involved in a real estate transaction, in essence when you purchase a property you are trading money for the title to the property. The escrow officer acts as a neutral third party. They hold the money and they hold the title to ensure that there's no tradeoff until all the pieces are in alignment; otherwise you could have a situation where somebody wound up getting cheated. The escrow officer is important and serves both buyer and seller impartially.

In most cases you have a lender that's also involved in the process, and the lender's role is generally the most unpredictable element of the transaction. If you talk to any experienced real estate agent they'll have more than their fair share of war stories of lenders who started causing problems in the 11th hour of a transaction.

This is the primary reason why cash offers are more attractive to sellers than financed offers. People who are not familiar with real estate often don't understand why cash means more because they think, "Well, wait a minute. In the end, if they're getting the money, what do they care whether it's the bank paying or whether I'm writing the check?"

The reason is because with a lender you never really know if the deal's going to close until the very end. There's an element of unpredictability with financed offers and this is why good communication between the lender and all parties is crucial to reducing the likelihood of any sort of problem or misunderstanding. The agent and the escrow officer should be dealing with the lender, making sure that the lender has everything they need in a timely fashion.

Next, there is an inspector who plays a very critical role in terms of determining what challenges there may be with the house. We can talk in more depth about that in a little bit, but suffice it to say this can be a critically important role in making sure that you're buying what you think you're buying, and that there won't be any surprises.

There's also an insurance agent involved, and this person makes sure that the property is insurable—critically important before consummating a transaction. In most closings, either buyer or seller will purchase a home warranty for the benefit of the new owner. It's a good thing to have in place as it offers everyone peace of mind.

In Arizona we don't typically have attorneys involved in the writing of the contract and the documents for most residential transactions. If a residential transaction is complex then there can be circumstances in which attorneys are involved, but in Arizona the agents are able to draft the offer documents, and then the escrow officer typically handles all documents drafted during escrow.

Arizona is a bit different with regard to the agent's role in the contract, so in most states there will be attorneys involved. When speaking about negotiations I stressed the importance of creating a contract that uses clear and simple language, making it easy for the other side to accept our offer. Well, this is where you flip into the opposite mode—investigating all details and every potential consequence to make sure that you're handling every contingency. The attorneys are experts at exploring every contingency and detail.

In sum, these are some of the main players that are involved in the process, and one of the things that I do to try to make life better for my clients is to vet these people so that when we have to bring in an outside resource, it's a trusted and strategic partner; it's not just someone from the Yellow Pages.

A good agent will know attorneys who have deep experience in relevant areas of law, and when I introduce my clients I make sure that each professional is experienced, reputable and an expert in their field. That's a substantial part of what I do as a real estate professional—I am constantly vetting people to make sure that the key services are well represented for my clients.

I know there are a lot of different parts and I've just said a lot, but I hope that clarifies it for you, Greg.

GREG

Alex, that really is a very long list. In your Action Guide you have a breakdown of all these different people and what they mean to the real estate transaction. With so many people and so many things going through the final stages of this process, what are some ways to control the process from our standpoint?

ALEX

Once again, this is where your agent should be earning their keep. I've got a whole system and methodology for handling a transaction. Once the offer's written, there's software that has every single document organized and everything is perfectly laid out on our side so that we know what's going on. We're also in regular communication with the title officer, who's going to be the person who's responsible for making sure that the money and the title all come together as they're supposed to.

The first time I bought a home it was a terrifying experience and I empathize with clients what clients are feeling. When I signed those closing documents the first time it seemed like the pile of pages was a foot high and they were taking my fingerprints and I was like, "Oh my gosh, what do they want, a blood sample next?" It was a taxing process that I didn't understand. Now I'm quite used to the process but I still remember what that was like, and I empathize with my clients as they go through it.

The easiest way to get through it is honestly to rely on your agent and to set up a good chain of communication. During this stage, establishing a standard of communication is key to maintaining a good relationship. It is critical to make clear how frequently you want your updates, because there are some people that want to know the minute anything happens of any significance, and then there are other people who just say, "I don't want to be bothered. You can give me a weekly update; just let me know anything important and otherwise I don't want to hear about it." The client and agent should decide together how often they plan to offer updates, whether these updates should come by email or phone, etc. This way the agent can meet their clients expectations and their client is clear about what to expect in terms of communication.

GREG

It sounds like the agent is really supposed to quarterback the whole process in this stage, But before we actually get to the closing table and start signing documents, something that needs to happen is the inspection. Let's talk about some of the high-level things that we need to know about the inspection process.

ALEX

Most people who are purchasing homes aren't experts in construction, maintenance and the various systems that make up the infrastructure of a house. There are really only two types of homes in the world: those that have problems that you can find, and those that have problems you haven't found. So they all have problems, and consequently I make a dedicated effort to work with inspectors who are very, very thorough and methodical.

It can cause a certain element of consternation for my clients when they start hearing about all kinds of worries that they had never previously considered. Hence I always try to preface the inspection by saying that I guarantee that the inspector is going to find some things wrong. It's better to hear all the problems up front than to learn about them days, weeks, or months after closing.

From the seller's standpoint the inspection period can be enlightening as well, because for the most part if you've been living in a house for a long time, you wouldn't have any reason to fix something unless it became an obvious problem. It's not as if you're going to be searching every crevice of your home with a flashlight to try to find every tiny problem. Typically, an owner only fixes something in their home when it's a nuisance.

Importantly, this is a point in time where you may reopen the negotiations, so that's another reason why inspection deserves serious attention. The inspection report can change the financial terms of the agreement if there are material problems that have been discovered. This is another phase where disagreement can potentially derail a deal, because if you can't get the buyer and the seller to agree upon what's significant and what should be fixed, then the deal can come unhinged.

Thus it's worth making sure you have an inspector who is not only thorough in the inspection that they perform, but also provides a report that is very clear. There is great variability in reports produced by inspectors, unfortunately. I expect to see a properly formatted document loaded with pictures, that clearly delineates significant problems versus minor issues. Too many inspectors provide a laundry list of problems with no context, which severely limits the utility of the report.

If you're presenting an inspection report to someone on the other side of the table, you want it to look professional and credible, so that you can get any and all reasonable concessions.

GREG

Alex, that's a really great overview of the inspection process. Something else that we need to think about that we often overlook at the end of the transaction process is title insurance. Let's talk about what title insurance is, and what we need to know about the title insurance process.

ALEX

Title insurance is there to, as the name implies, insure your title. What that means is this: when you're taking ownership of a piece of property, you're getting ownership of that title, and you want some insurance to be certain that the little piece of paper you're getting is worth all the money you are paying.

There can be things that would break the so-called chain of title, and that's why you need insurance. Over the years, title to a property has been passed through many hands and there can be encumbrances that cloud your right to have clear ownership of that property. Often, these are not things that you would know about. They could be buried deep in the past and sometimes they come out of the woodwork, so to speak. Your title insurance protects you in the event this happens.

Let me give you an example of the value of title insurance. In Arizona there's a lot of property that has substantial mineral rights. It's common for mineral rights to get separated from the land. Once, I owned several hundred acres of land where some mineral rights had been sold unbeknownst to me, and some guy comes out of the woodwork after I took ownership. The fact that he had this claim was not disclosed at the time I purchased the land, and this was not something that the seller was aware of either. So this legitimate claim could have caused a big problem, but I had title insurance. So it became the title company's responsibility to pay that claim, and that's exactly what happened.

In the case of a home, these types of things are pretty rare because in most urban areas the title's going to be clean and well-established. Nevertheless you want to make sure you have that insurance for the same reason you want car insurance, home insurance or health insurance: just in case.

There's another thing that I'd like to talk about, Greg, which is how one holds title. Do we have time to give some thought to that?

GREG

Yes, I think this is really important, so please spend a few minutes talking about how this is different from just the title insurance process.

ALEX

Insurance reimburses you if there are any problems with the title, but how you hold title is a determination of literally who or what owns the property. It astounds me how little effort is often put into making this critical decision.

It's particularly important when it comes to luxury property because if you are buying an expensive home, that's making an advertisement that you have substantial financial means. Any attorney who sues people will tell you that the people who get sued are the people who have deep pockets. Lawyers aren't stupid; they don't sue people who don't have money to pay judgments.

So the first thing that a lawyer's looking for before they sue anyone is: does this person have money to pay out if they win? When you buy an expensive home you are advertising to the world that you have substantial financial means, and that makes you a target.

You want to protect yourself, especially if you're buying with cash and you're going to have a lot of equity. It's important you're holding title in a way that allows you to protect your investment. I always have this discussion with my clients to make sure that they're aware this is something that they should carefully consider—particularly in the luxury segment.

In Arizona we have the *Arizona Republic* as our largest newspaper, and they print the home sales that were the largest of the week. So every week I see it: the names and the dollar figures and the locations of homes that are being sold, and I think this is outrageous. The last thing I would want if I bought a multi-million dollar property would be to have it listed in the newspaper with, "Hey, here I am! I've got all this money! Come find me!" It's crazy, but people don't spend the time to prevent this.

I have this conversation with my clients, and I strongly advise them to meet with an attorney that specializes in asset protection.

This is why I have as one of my strategic partners an asset protection attorney who does nothing but asset protection; literally nothing else—he's an expert and true specialist in asset protection. What he tells me is that *half of his work is fixing the mistakes of other attorneys*. So there are many wealthy people out there who think they are protected and they are not—and that's even worse than not being protected at all, because you've paid money and made the effort and have zero protection to show for it.

The people that come into his office are not unsophisticated, they are millionaires. Hence, I always advise my clients to at least take an hour of their time to meet with an asset protection attorney, a specialist, to discuss this matter, because it's a multi-million dollar asset that they're either buying now or with appreciation will be worth many millions someday. They should take every step to protect their investment.

One of the most common misconceptions is that revocable trusts can be used to protect assets. You would not believe how many millionaires falsely believe this. The fact is that that revocable trusts are estate planning tools—they do *not* protect your assets while you are alive. If a judge orders you to revoke the trust, you must do so, and then it's "open season" on those assets. Hence, irrevocable trusts are valuable for protecting assets while you are alive, not revocable trusts.

Given all the misconceptions and the huge amount of money at stake, this is something that needs to be given more attention. I go to great lengths to protect my clients and to make sure that they have resources at their disposal to help protect their investment.

GREG

Alex, this just goes to show the level of depth and value that you bring to the real estate transaction process. It's clear that you care about helping clients get the results that they desire.

Brian Tracy earlier spoke in detail about assets, and your assets in running a business. Based on some of your own experiences, what are some of the best ways to protect our assets during the home buying and selling process?

ALEX

Once again, meeting with an attorney who specializes in asset protection is important. It is also important for you to meet with your financial advisor and to look at your overall financial picture to understand where your real estate asset fits in with the rest of your portfolio.

For instance, a lot of times people think, "Okay, I've got X amount of dollars parked with my stockbroker," and in their mind that's entirely separate from their real estate. Well, that's true in one sense, but it's really not true, because what if your stockbroker thinks that REIT's (Real Estate Investment Trusts) are a great place to be and he's got you heavily invested in REIT's.

While REIT's may be a great investment, your advisor may not realize that a huge portion of your overall net worth is already in real estate in the form of a house that you own. It's therefore important to make sure that when you make the decision to invest in an expensive home that you tell your advisor to adjust your exposure to real estate accordingly. Conversely, if you are downsizing, you are effectively reducing your exposure to real estate and your financial advisor should know that as well.

Also, of course, you want to bring in your accountant to understand the tax implications, and consult your estate planning attorney. Both tax and estate rules are constantly changing, so it's important to be in close contact with these advisors.

These are important things to do, particularly when purchasing a home that you're going to be in for the long term. That could be 10 or 20 years or more, and so much the better that you do everything correctly in the beginning and don't have to worry about it again because you've got all the pieces of the puzzle in place. I'm happy to help my clients vet and qualify people to work with them on these important matters.

Many of the clients that come to me already have financial advisors and estate planners and so forth, so I just say to them, "Make sure that you're keeping those folks in the loop. When they make your financial plan for the following year they can take that into account, make sure that it's not some quantity that's left off their data."

Those are some of the key things, Greg. It's important to understand how one financial decision impacts your overall financial situation and your portfolio and to involve experts in every stage of the process to protect yourself, your assets and your investment.

GREG

Yes, again, that's very powerful information, and so important to keep all of these people in the loop during this process. You know, Alex, throughout this entire program we've been leading up to the topic we're about to discuss, and that's closing day.

Let's imagine we're finally at closing day. We've found our expert advisor agent, we have gone through the process, we've negotiated, we're going through the little things and all the pieces that need to come together. Now we're at a very exciting day, and this day brings a lot of emotion to the surface.

I was hoping you could walk us through a closing day and note some of the things that we need to pay attention to throughout the final stages of the transaction.

ALEX

We discussed earlier how it's very common for people to get cold feet late in the game and to worry that they've made the wrong decision. Usually by the time closing day happens everybody's already somewhat locked in—you can't just walk away from the transaction without substantial consequences. As an agent I try to allow the weight of evidence and information to help them feel good about what's been happening and what is about to happen at closing.

By the time we get to closing, I've provided a lot of information about what's going on in the marketplace and about what the other options may be. I've guided them to strategic partners and advisors and during consultations with these experts they've received quality information and opinions from a lot of people apart from me.

There's an element of risk involved with any transaction. To quote J.P. Morgan: "Markets will continue to fluctuate." As we've seen in recent years, the real estate market certainly does fluctuate. Nothing is guaranteed. But by the time closing happens, an agent that has done his/her job has gone to every length possible to cover all the bases. In other words, nobody can predict the future, but we can work hard and work smart to stack the deck in our client's favor as much as possible.

It is nerve-wracking to relocate your belongings and your family. There's a lot to do, and it can be overwhelming when the moment finally arrives. Buyers should try to focus on what they've accomplished and I encourage them to be excited about closing and everything the future holds. They've been dreaming about their home, the furniture they're going to buy and every other detail that goes along with moving. It's time to stop dreaming and embrace the reality that they have earned.

Sellers have an opportunity to reflect on their achievement too. They've completed a big sale and they can now move on to the next phase of their life.

Typically by the time we get to the day of closing it's a pretty smooth process. It's comforting for my clients to fall back on all of the experts and information that have been provided along the way, so they feel secure signing on the dotted line.

GREG

Now, Alex, when all is said and done and we've signed the papers, when we reflect on the process, what should we be thinking about when it comes to the relationship that we have with our real estate agent?

ALEX

When you get to closing and all is done, there's usually a sense of joy and relief, and often times people may not even recognize all moving parts that got them there. When it's all done, it's nice to know that you have somebody there who's had your back.

I usually find that on closing day people are pretty thrilled, and it's a wonderful privilege to share in their joy. One of the most rewarding parts of my job is helping people through a life transition. That's really what this is: a life transition, and not just a transaction.

I do work with investor clients, I've done a lot of investments myself, and I certainly enjoy that part of the work—making a lot of money for people is thrilling in its own right. From an emotional standpoint, there's nothing quite like helping people transition into a new stage in their lives.

So working with people who are looking to buy or sell a luxury home is really thrilling, because I know that I'm having an impact on their lives, that in many cases may last a decade or more.

It's really wonderful, and I enjoy it. If I do my job right it's a pretty darn great experience for them as well, and I've got a lot of clients who've told me that. It keeps me motivated to be at the top of my game.

GREG

Alex, that's great that you can provide this for your clients. As we begin to wrap up this program I'd like to talk about the working relationship that you have with your clients.

If, after going through this program, someone says to himself or herself: "You know what? I would love to have Alex on my side, on my team, to guide us through this process and to be that expert and that advisor, that person who's going to get us what we want." Talk about how that relationship starts with you. What steps can someone take to work with you?

ALEX

Well, I encourage people to reach out to me and ask me any questions they have.

I also encourage people to get some of my free resources so

they can become better educated on the process, whether it's a buyer's guide or information about what they can do to prepare for selling their home, those are all free resources that I'm happy to provide to people.

Of course, if they'd like information on the areas that I work in, Paradise Valley, Scottsdale, and Phoenix then I can provide a lot of detailed information specific to that marketplace. If they're looking in other areas of Arizona I may be able to direct them to an expert in that area. In any case, I'm here to help and I welcome anyone to reach out to me to say hello, ask questions or just to chat.

The best way for people to get started with any of these resources, or to contact me about Arizona real estate, would be to sign up for my newsletter at *ParadiseValleyNewsletter. com.* They'll receive a weekly update, as well as my contact information if they'd like to speak directly.

GREG

Alex, I want to thank you for providing those resources to your community and for opening up that line of communication. Again, the resources to get in touch with Alex are in your Action Guide: email address, phone number, the website where you can get some of these free resources, the buyer's guide and the information about Paradise Valley and Scottsdale to help you make an informed buying decision and to get a real estate agent who is on your side—someone that is looking out for you.

Alex, I want to thank you for taking the time out of your busy schedule to share this information in an effort to prepare buyers and sellers. I think your insight will help individuals entering this marketplace to feel more comfortable.

ALEX

Thanks, Greg. It was really an honor to be here, and I appreciate you taking the time.

GREG

Definitely, and again, please go back through the different modules, go through your Action Guide, and take action, because you're going to get the best results when you take the information that Alex has laid out for you—ask the questions he has recommended, utilize the resources he has provided, and take advantage of everything that he has put together in this package as you work toward finding your next home.

I do want to thank you for going through this program. Alex and I both want to hear from you as you purchase your next home to talk about the difference that this information made. Thanks again for listening, and we will talk to you again soon.

SUMMARY

REAL ESTATE AGENT

The agent will be coordinating the many people involved in closing the transaction. Establish how often you want updates from your agent, and whether you prefer email or phone, so that you'll be in the loop without getting overwhelmed. Also, ask your agent for recommendations of other professionals with whom they have worked such as home inspectors, attorneys, etc.

HOME INSPECTOR

The home inspector's report is critical to understanding the property and negotiating concessions based on material problems with the structure. Don't settle for a flimsy report, demand one that has lots of photos and is organized in a way that allows you to quickly determine what's important from what's inconsequential.

ESCROW OFFICER

The escrow officer acts as a neutral third party, protecting money and title until the day of closing. Usually they will also be responsible for issuing title insurance. The most important, and often overlooked person in the transaction, they are the gatekeeper of all documents for the transaction.

LENDER

The lender's role is very significant and can be among the most challenging elements of the transaction. Some lenders make requests and changes at the 11th hour, so it's important to work with a lender who has a track record of doing what they say and funding on time.

INSURANCE AGENT

Get quotes on insurance as early in the process as possible, so you can avoid any unpleasant surprises. If a property has a history of substantial claims, this could make insurance expensive or even impossible to obtain.

FINANCIAL ADVISOR AND CPA

Keep your financial advisor and CPA informed, so that you can rest assured you're avoiding unpleasant tax or financial implications with your home transaction.

ATTORNEY

How will you take title to the property? Make sure that you are protecting your home by properly structuring the transaction at closing. An asset protection attorney can review options such as irrevocable trusts that may provide greater protection and privacy than closing in your own name.

SECTION 2

THE BUSINESS OF BUSINESS

CHAPTER 4:

BUSINESS SUCCESS SECRETS

GREG

Hi, this is Greg Rollett and today I'm joined by a very special guest. We're very privileged to have the legendary Brian Tracy joining us today as we're going to be talking about how your business can really survive and thrive in today's economy.

Brian, over the course of this program we're going to be talking about both your experience in your own business and with businesses that you've been able to help become more successful over the years.

A lot of people know your background as a sales and leadership trainer and they might not see the experience you have in the business world. I'd really love to open up this conversation by talking about the journey that you've had both in your own business and through helping others.

BRIAN

When I started off my career I came from a poor family. I did poorly in school, and my first business was selling soap when I was ten years old, from door to door. I learned something there that changed my life in business forever: I would knock on doors and I would say, "I'm selling soap to go to YMCA camp. Would you like to buy a box?" and they'd say "No. No, thank you; not interested. Don't want it, can't use it, can't afford it."

Then one day, just by accident, and very often business people have an accident and something works and it changes their business.

By accident, I said, "I'm Brian Tracy, I'm selling Rosamel beauty soap, but it's strictly for beautiful women," and then I stopped.

All the resistance disappeared. She said, "Well, it wouldn't be for me." I said, "Oh, yes, it would." She said, "Well, then I'll take a box," and she took a box, and I began selling soap like you cannot imagine. I sold more soap than almost all the other kids in the campaign put together.

I sold enough soap for myself and thirteen other kids to go to YMCA camp; I broke every record in the industry. I could sell soap to virtually every single person I spoke to. If I was speaking to a man, I'd say, "It's strictly for handsome men."

It's strictly for beautiful women. My point is this: it is the psychology of the selling. It is the emotional impact; it's the transformation that takes place in the person's life or work that causes a person to buy or not buy your product or service, and if you cannot connect with that, people will say, "Don't want it, don't need it, can't use it. I'm not interested." But if you can connect with that, you can sell your product or service all day long.

GREG

I love that. Throughout this program we're going to talk about how you've transitioned from selling soap to building an international company working with millions of people all around the world and I think that's going to add some great experience and great lessons that business owners can really derive from.

Now, I want to talk about what a successful business looks like. I'm sure it's changed from selling soap to running the company that you guys have now, so in your mind, what are some of the characteristics that make a business successful in today's economy?

BRIAN

If you build a building, you always start with the foundation. And what is the foundation? The purpose of a business is not to make a profit; the purpose of a business is to create and keep a customer. Of all the focus of everyone in the business, 80% has to be on customer creation, and the other 20% has to be on customer keeping: taking such good care of your customers after the sale.

So the purpose of a business is to create and keep a customer; that's the 80%, what we call the point of the spear. The question is: what is the measure of a successful business? The answer is customer satisfaction. The customer uses the product and is happy that they decided to buy your product or service.

So what is the measure of customer satisfaction? The answer is repeat business. The customer buys it and is so happy they buy it again and tell their friends. Here's the final, ultimate- and this is breakthrough stuff- the ultimate of successful business is that customers recommend you enthusiastically to others and say, "You've got to buy this product or service like I did."

So your customers become your best salespeople, your advocates. The key to all of this, the foundation, is creating a great product or service that makes people happy that causes them to buy again and causes them to enthusiastically tell their friends, and that has to be the central focal purpose of everything you do in business.

GREG

I think that's really important, and right now I really encourage you to have your Action Guides in front of you. I encourage you to think about your existing products and services and go through them and see the customer experience the entire way through the funnel from the time someone learns about your product to when they buy the product to when they're using the product, because there's different customer experiences for each level of involvement with the product and I think that's really, really important, moving forward in this program.

One thing that I think business owners need to really stop and think about, especially if their business might be struggling in today's economy, they need to stop and really assess where they are in the marketplace, wouldn't you agree?

BRIAN

Yes. One of the most important things that we teach in our programs is what is called "Zero-Based Thinking". Zero-Based Thinking is one of the greatest of all personal and business concepts.

It says that you stop on a regular basis, like time-out, stop, and you ask yourself this question: "Is there anything that I am doing today that, knowing what I now know in the current market, I would not start up again today?

"Is there any product or service that I'm offering that knowing what I now know, I would bring to the market? Is there any process, any expenditure, any activity in my business that knowing what I now know, I would not start again if I had to do it over? Is there any person that I've hired or I'm working with or working for or partnering with who, knowing what I now know, I would not get involved with again?"

If the answer is no, the next question is, "How do I get out of this and how fast?" Slam on the brakes, because here's the discovery: once the answer comes back "No", the situation is not savable. It's the most amazing thing; you can't go back and adjust it and modify it.

If you say, "No, I would not start this or get into this or hire this person again," it's too late to save it. The only question is: Do you have the courage and do you have the resolution to stop it and start using your time and your resources in better areas?

GREG

I think that's really important to make that stop now and not let it continue as you go. Once we've seen that, we're starting to assess our business and we're answering the questions you just asked. I think the next step, moving forward, is setting real, actionable goals for the business.

I know you have some great theories and strategies and tactics to help business owners set some goals. Once we've kind of looked back and we've answered some questions, we've found some problem areas in our business, how do we set goals moving forward?

BRIAN

There are two ways to set business goals. What most people do is they set sales goals, and your sales goals have to be broken down. First of all you say, "I want to sell this amount in this year," and your business planning, your market planning, your research, is all aimed at giving you realistic numbers of how much you can actually sell.

Everything costs twice as much and takes three times as long in business. Let me repeat: everything costs twice as much and takes three times as long. So if you do really good business planning- conservative, thoughtful, based on research- which most people don't- even then, it's going to cost twice as much and take three times as long, so you have to build that into your calculations.

People say, "I want to sell this much in this year." Well, then they have to break it down to how much they want to sell each month. Then you have to break it down to how much you have to sell each day, and what some people do is break it down into how much you have to sell each hour.

Think of QVC; QVC actually breaks it down to how much they sell each minute.

I've been on QVC. There are two ways to be on QVC, and I did not know the right way. So I started talking about my product and how good it was and everything else, and the numbers didn't move.

They jerked me and within 30 minutes I was off of QVC, and I've never been invited back. However, I went onto another television channel later, and I had a morning and an afternoon slot. In the morning slot I did the same thing with QVC; how good my product is and how nice it is and everything else, and the sales were average.

But they had me scheduled for the evening slot, so they gave me one more chance. I went back to my hotel and I turned my whole sales presentation around and I focused it totally on the difference my product will make in your life: how it will improve your life and your work and your health and your happiness and your income and your relationships and everything else.

I went back and I didn't even talk about my product; I just talked about benefit, benefit, benefit, benefit, benefit, and the phones fell off the hook. We sold thousands and thousands of dollars worth of product, and I realized: my God, it's Rosamel beauty soap again! Nobody cares about what your product is; they only care what it does.

So when you start to plan out what you want to sell you have to focus on: what does my product do and how many people can it do that for? Then you have to work out how much it's going to cost you to achieve those sales goals and how much will be left over at the end of the day.

GREG

I think that's really important and I love some of the things you just said in there. I think it, again, goes back to the benefit of what your product can do, and that's really important. It goes back to assessing competition and thinking about your business as a whole, instead of just having the blinders on, thinking, "Well, I make soap."

That's really, really important. What I encourage you guys to do right now is in your Action Guides you have a section where you can start to create your own goals, whether it's sales goals, different numbers, production goals that you want to do, and I encourage you to spend a few minutes going through that because it's really, really important to set these goals.

After you've set these goals, rip that page out of your Action Guide and paste it up right next to your computer or next to the whiteboard near your conference table, wherever you need to see it, because you really need to revisit these things on a regular basis, right?

BRIAN

Right. There's a method that you can use that has made more people rich, in business especially, than any other creative thinking method ever discovered. I use it all the time and it's made me rich. It's very simply called the 20-Idea Method. Sometimes we call it Mind-Storming, where you actually focus on bringing out the best thoughts in your own mind.

We do it with groups of business owners, but also we encourage people to do it alone. What you do is you take your goal or problem and you write it in the form of a question at the top of the page.

For example, your goal is to sell x number of dollars worth of product in one year or one month. Then what you do is say, "How can I sell this amount of product by this date?" Very specific question. Then you generate 20 ideas.

You discipline yourself to keep writing until you have at least 20 ideas; sometimes I'll get to 25 or 35. The first time you do this will be very hard, but you keep saying, "I could do this and I could do that and I could do this. I could promote here; I could cut here; I could discount there. I could joint venture with this; I could do strategic alliance here."

You keep writing down every single thing that you could think of to achieve that sales goal, and the most amazing darn thing- and I just did this exercise for myself two days ago on a project that I'm working on- is answer number 20 is often the breakthrough answer that will make you rich, not 19.

People quit after 5 or 6 or 8 or 10 answers because your mind will dry up, but keep pushing, keep squeezing your brain, because you've got the information in there. The 20th answer, and I've seen this for more than 25 years, often transforms people's lives and takes them from rags to riches.

Therefore, 20 ideas. 20 ideas to achieve your sales goals; 20 ideas to achieve your profitability goals. 20 ideas. If you want to have some fun, do it with a group of people and have them throw out ideas.

I worked at a company once—I've got to tell you this great story—their sales were about 20 million a year. Their goal was, over the next two years, to get to 25 million. So I took 17 executives through the Mind-Storming process and we wrote all the answers on flip charts and put them up around the room.

They were skeptical, but they came up with 37 answers; 37 answers to increase their sales by 25 to 50%. Five years later their sales were $104 million. They literally blew the doors off the entire industry, and it was all attributable to the ideas generated in this once session.

Does it work? Yes. The only thing I ask you to do is try it out, and the true measure of how serious you are about succeeding in business is if you hear a good idea, you try it once.

Most people won't try an idea the first time. They've always got to reason. "Oh, I'm too busy, and I don't know if it'll work," and so on. I'm telling you, it works, so give it a try.

Write down your most important business question or problem as a question, and write down 20 answers. Then take action on at least one of those immediately.

GREG

That's a take-action item right now. That might be a pause and come back and visit us in a few minutes. It really does come down to taking action if you want to see the results that you really want to see in your business.

Go ahead; you guys have that exercise and I really want you to take advantage of it because it's worked for Brian, it's worked for your businesses. Just hearing that story; that's really just incredible.

As we grow from that, we've talked about how, with your soap, it was about having the benefits: what's the benefit of the product? That it's only for beautiful women or handsome men or whatever the case is.

Part of that in this economy is a lot of businesses are in the price war, the lowest price war, and that's not the business that we want to be in. We don't want to be seen as a commodity, as a low-price strategy.

I think having the benefits that you were talking about helps you get out of that. How do we transition from the low-price business to getting into get a benefit-driven business where we can get the prices and the affluent customers that are really going to make a difference in our business?

BRIAN

Today it's interesting; the high-price stores, products, and services—Mercedes-Benz, Rolls Royces, Rolex watches—they're selling out of stock.

People say you have to cut prices; you only have to cut prices if you can't think of any other reason for people to buy your product or service.

What you're talking about is you talk about the benefit. We talk about what is called a Unique Selling Proposition, a USP, and this is the one reason why people should want to buy your product or service more than any other product or service that's available. You have to be crystal clear about that.

What you do is you offer a benefit that is really, really desirable. Many people say, "This is a great benefit because it'll do this and it'll do that," but the feature is not a benefit. A benefit is a result, and out comes a transformation that will take place in the life or work of the person that is worth paying money for.

What you do is you offer them this benefit. You say, "If you use my product, this is what you'll enjoy. You will become a beautiful woman, a handsome man." People don't care about the means; all they care about is the end.

A good friend of mine has a wonderful way of putting it: if you're selling a vacation, you sell the destination, not the airplane. Most people spend 90% of their time selling the airplane, the travel, the arrangements, the hotel you stay in, the transportation from the hotel, and so on and so forth.

No! People want to know about the warm beaches and the palm trees and the lovely ocean. So you spend 90% of your time talking about the benefit or result that the person will enjoy.

You talk about the pleasure, the difference. People don't buy life insurance; they buy peace of mind. People don't buy investments; they buy long-term security for themselves and your family.

You've got to think: what is the ultimate outcome or result or benefit, and if you buy my product, I promise you, you will get this benefit in spades, and I'll guarantee it. If your product or service is good, people will guarantee it.

You're using an iPad; if you bought that iPad and it didn't work, they would snatch it out of your hand and replace it with a brand-new iPad and an apology, and probably several upgrades and a bonus, and send you a note as well because they take the functionality, the working of their product, the delivery of the promise so seriously, the same as every single successful company whether it's Amazon or Mercedes-Benz or Lexus or anything else. They promise you a benefit that will have an impact on your life, and they stand behind it 100%.

GREG

I think that goes back—and we're hearing some themes recurring over and over again—it also goes back to customer experience when you're driving that benefit and how you're talking about Apple and even Amazon and Mercedes-Benz; it's a total customer experience that goes to the benefit, but it also follows through on that benefit.

BRIAN

Yes. This is something I'm really adamant about; I teach it all the time. I speak to about 250,000 people a year; I speak to thousands of business owners.

Here's something that's so important, and the measure of your success is simply this: how many people, after using your product or service, go, "Jeez! This is a great product! This is a great service!" If they don't say that, then you have to go back to the drawing boards and keep working and increasing the percentage of users who say, "Jeez, this is a great product!"

Have you ever been to a great restaurant and you walk out of that restaurant and you say, "Boy, that was a great restaurant! That was a great dinner! Those are great people."?

Every place that people go back to over and over again, when they describe it to others, they say, "There are really great people there. Great products; great services." The problem, Greg, is too many people are trying to sell average, and sometimes not even average products, by trying to find a gimmick.

They're trying to find a trick, they're trying to find some way to con people into buying a lousy product, a product that they'll only buy once, whereas all successful businesses, going back to my basic model, focus on making their customers so happy in delivering the promise that the customers say, "This is a great product!" and they want to buy it again and they want to bring their friends.

"You've got to come; I'm going to take you to this restaurant." "You've got to see this movie! This movie's incredible; I'll buy you a ticket." That's the kind of experience that you want your customers to have, and if they have that, you can charge almost anything you want and your business will grow and grow and grow.

GREG

I love that and it makes a whole lot of sense. Again, it's that customer experience. We're hearing recurring themes throughout this first part.

We've really been talking about what makes a business successful in today's economy, and in the last part of this first section I wanted to talk about your team because the team members really make a difference in your business being successful or not, either as a solo entrepreneur or a small-business owner as a small team, the team is really important.

Even in your business where you're out there, you're doing the speaking; you're doing the training; you've developed a team as well that really keeps the machine moving. Can you talk about how you've been able to build a team that you can trust and rely on while you're on the road or you're working with different groups?

BRIAN

First of all, hiring somebody to help you, to back you up, is very similar to getting married. You just don't rush into it; you just don't meet a person and say, "Hey, you look good. Let's get married!" What you do is you have to go slow, and when you start your business, by the way, you're going to make a lot of mistakes.

You're going to have a revolving door. The average turnover for a small business is about 200% a year, and the reason for that is hiring is not only a skill that takes a lot of experience, but also there are a lot of people out there who have only one skill, and that's interviewing well for a job.

So they'll seem nice and cheerful and friendly and they'll have a nice curriculum vitæ of their skills and so on. Within 24 to 48 hours you'll realize this person can't find their bum with both hands. So we see this all the time, so this is one of the things I recommend: we're always hiring.

We have about 15, 16 people and we have low turnover; about

10 or 12 of the people have been there 5 or 10 years, but we do have new people. One of the things I teach is called the law of three.

The law of three in this says interview a person that you like at least three times, then interview that person in three places and have that person interviewed by three other people.

If you take the law of three, what I say is interview at least three people for the job and pick one you like, interview that person at least three times, interview them in three places; don't sit in your same office, same chair. Take them across the street to McDonald's and buy them a cup of coffee.

I once was interviewed by a very wealthy man worth $800 million, and I didn't even know it was an interview. He invited me to come out with him to his ranch; he had a ranch outside of town. We just walked around and he showed his cattle and he showed me other things.

We walked around and I commented and he asked me little questions about my background and so on and so forth. Afterwards we came back to the house and he said, "Okay, the job is yours." I didn't even realize that was a job interview.

He was just checking to see how I would behave and how I treated other people at the ranch and whether I opened the gate and things like that. He was just kind of watching. I've been interviewed like this before by senior people; they take you for a walk and just talk about general things.

So interview them three times. Now, here's the key: before you hire anybody, have that person interviewed by at least three people other than yourself. You say, "I'm a little person. I don't have a big business." Well, have your wife interview.

Everybody has to be interviewed by my wife, by the way, because women have tremendous sense for whether a person will work out right or wrong. Have your friend who works in your other business interview this person.

Have your accountant interview this person. Have somebody else; three people. Never trust your own judgment to hire when you're a business builder because you're emotional, you're impetuous, you're busy, you're distracted.

You look upon hiring as something you've just got to get over with. Have three other people talk to the person, and then say, "What do you think?" If the consensus is 100%, hire them. If one person says no, don't hire them.

Remember, it's easier not to hire a person than to hire a person and have to wrestle and fight with them and then get rid of them and then get sued by them and all the darn things that can happen to you. Hire slow; we say "Hire slow, fire fast".

GREG

It's a good motto to work with. Building on that, now that you've gone through this hiring process, let's talk about how beneficial your team is to your business.

BRIAN

I have a team, as I say, of about 15 people. Each one of them, as a matter of fact, has been hired through this process; they all know how to use this process, so they actually hire the people under them.

There are about four or five people in my office who do hiring, which is an interesting point, by the way. In any company there are three or four people who have the capacity to hire a person.

That's one of the things, if you can avoid it, by all means do it: when my people hire somebody, I'm the last person to pass judgment. They introduce the person to me after they've been vetted three times at three places by three people.

So now you have a person in place. Then the most important word for business success is clarity. Clarity: each person must know exactly what it is that you want them to do and exactly why you want them to do it.

If you can give them a clear 'why', they'll be very creative in the 'what' and the 'how'. Then what you do is you keep giving and delegating tasks to people that free you up to do the things that pay even more. You always use another factor we call 'hourly rate', and you say, "Calculate your desired hourly rate."

If you want to earn $50,000 a year your desired hourly rate is $25. If you want to earn $100,000 a year your desired hourly rate is $50; that's your annual income divided by 2,000 hours, the average number of hours an entrepreneur works.

Then you say, "All right, I want to earn $25 an hour, so that means I cannot do $10 an hour work. I can't do typing; I can't do checking email; I can't read the paper or make coffee or photocopies."

What you do is as soon as you determine this is what you want to earn, then what you do is you hire anyone else who can do that at a lower hourly rate than you desire to free up your time for doing things that only you can do.

GREG

That's really, really powerful. I like that strategy a lot. What I want to do now is I want to bring this first section and really wrap it up. We've been talking about what really makes a successful business in today's economy.

We've heard some really great recurring themes: it's the customer experience, it's the benefit your product brings to the marketplace, it's about hiring great people that are going to make an impact and free you up to do the things that are going to allow you to grow your business.

Let's talk to the business owners that might be struggling a little bit that are going through this program. What is the first thing, first action, that you would tell them to do to really take that direction to go from where they are now to where they want to go?

BRIAN

First of all, realize that all business owners are struggling. I'm a business owner; I'm struggling. One of the things that I learned many years ago, which is one of the great business concepts, is called the strategic business unit concept.

That's where you take the products and services that you have and divide them into specific units. For example, we have several seminars that we offer; we have several programs and seminars that we give; we have a series of products that we sell online.

What we do is we look upon each of them almost like a separate mini-business; like a separate strategic business unit. Then we have a mini business plan for each one rather than having them all together and everybody's doing a little bit of this and a little bit of that.

You think through zero-based thinking; if you were not now offering this product, would you bring it to the market? If the answer ever pops up 'no', then discontinue it. Perhaps the most important quality for business success in the 21st century, according to the Manager Institute, is flexibility.

Flexibility; be flexible. Realize that almost every decision you make will turn out to be wrong in the fullness of time, 70% or more; every product or service or marketing or advertising decision.

It may be right when you initiate, but that's questionable; but it'll turn out to be wrong because the market will change, so be flexible. Be willing to abandon things that aren't working.

The only questions you ask are: Does it work? Is it working? *Wall Street Journal* today said the most important thing an entrepreneur does is realize that if the customer is not buying it, stop selling it.

Don't beat your head against the wall just so it feels good when you stop.

Peter Drucker once said the greatest problem in business is managerial ego. We bring our product to the market, we invest our egos in it, we invest our time, our heart, we tell everybody it is and how wonderful it is, but like the story about the dog food, the dogs don't like it.

If customers don't like it, they don't want to buy it, they argue with you about price, they bring it back, move on to something else. What's the most successful high-tech company in the world today? It's Apple.

Do you remember Apple's NeXT Computer? Do you remember its tablet computer? They brought it out, it seemed like a good idea at the time, it bombed in the market; they just pulled it off the market and moved on.

You don't see them trying to keep on selling something that customers don't like. So be really flexible, be adaptable, adjust to the realities of the market, and be willing to try something new. Try to make your product faster, better, easier to use, cheaper; try different forms of advertising.

The most important thing that you need to know is if you could narrow it down and say to your customer, "You'll only get one benefit: this is the primary benefit." Let me rephrase it: "You'll get many others, but this is the one benefit, more than anything else, that you will get if you use my product or service."

Can you be absolutely crystal clear about that benefit, and then can you guarantee that your customer will get that benefit? If you can't be clear about the benefit, you need to be clear. If you can't guarantee it, take the product off the market.

I work with one of the biggest MLM companies in the world. They're very successful; very high-quality products. Every year they take product off the market because exhaustive research shows that the product is good, but it's not the best, so they just take it off the market and they discontinue it.

People say, "But I like that product! I like that product," including myself. People say, "Yes, but it doesn't meet our standards of being really excellent, so we've decided to discontinue it and focus only on those things that we can quite confidently say are really excellent."

A critical point is Aristotle said that the ultimate aim of all of human activity is to be happy. Happiness is the one thing that we all strive for. The only question is how good we are at achieving our own happiness.

Even Ayn Rand said this in her philosophy of Objectivism. Your job is to make your customers happy, and the whole focus is "How can I make my customers happy? How can I make them happier than my competitors? How can I make them so happy that they buy from me and buy it again and tell their friends?"

So whenever you're having challenges in the market, and there are always sales challenges, revenue challenges, pull back and say, "Wait a minute. For me to be successful, I've got to make people happy."

I'll give you a great story: Jim Collins' bestselling book *Good to Great* examined over 1,100 businesses and isolated several businesses that had been good for a long time and then became great businesses.

One of them was a company that realized—this was a Fortune 500 company, multi-billion dollar company—that the competition was so tough in their industry that they could never be the best in their industry, and by the best it means that you want to be in the top 10% of your industry.

They could never be the best, so they took a great big deep breath and they decided to sell off their company; sell off the factories and sell off the distribution facilities and sell off the distribution facilities and sell off the manufacturing and sell off everything and take the money and invest it in a new business where they could be the best in the industry, and they did.

Everybody said, "You must be crazy!" Their stock took a terrible beating in the stock market. Today it's one of the most respected, most profitable companies in the world because they had the courage to recognize that we cannot be excellent in this area; we can only be a "me too" product.

If you're a "me too" product, you have to sell solely by lowing your price and by gimmicks and by making claims that aren't true, and then by dodging customer phone calls and everything else. But if the product is great, people will line up.

Somebody said to me the other day, "My product is so good there's no competition." I said, "That's really incredible." This is a business owner, and I said, "That's really incredible. So, there must be a lineup of people around the block every morning when you get to work waiting for your services because they're so good," and he went, "Huh?"

I said, "There's no lineup? Well, that means that your product is not the best product. It's not the irreplaceable product. Your product's available; look in the Yellow Pages. Your product's available from 50 other companies."

He wrote back to me and he said that was the biggest shock of his life. He's been walking around telling everybody that his product is so unique and good it's the best in the business, and he realized that if it was the best in the business his phone would be falling off the hook; his waiting room would be jammed.

People would be lined up in the streets. The parking lot would be full. People would be throwing checks at him over the heads of other people if his product was that good. So don't fool yourself.

GREG

Right. Don't let the ego get in the way; be flexible. Brian's just shared with you some great wisdom, tips, and strategies of what a successful business looks like in today's economy, and I encourage you to go back and go through your Action Guide.

Look at all the things that you can do with your own products and services and with your team to make your products great, to make your customer experience a great place from the time that they learn about your product to the time they buy it to the time that they use it.

When we come back here in part two we're going to be talking about building your brand and your brand both as a business owner and through your business. Thanks again for listening to part one and we'll see you again in part two.

SUMMARY

ZERO-BASED THINKING

On a regular basis, ask yourself this question: "Is there anything that I am doing today that, knowing what I now know in the current market, I would not start up again today?" If the answer is no, the next question is, "How do I get out of this and how fast?"

If you say, "No, I would not start this or get into this or hire this person again," it's too late to save it. The only question is: Do you have the courage and do you have the resolution to stop it and start using your time and your resources in better areas?

If you can't come up with 5 benefits for your product, rethink the product. How can you make it better, faster, cheaper or easier to use? Analyze all your products this way.

MIND STORMING

If your goal is to sell x number of dollars worth of product then ask yourself "How can I sell this amount of product by this date?" Then you generate 20 ideas. Discipline yourself to keep writing until you have at least 20 ideas.

Keep writing down every single thing that comes to mind— answer number 20 is often the breakthrough answer that will make you rich, not 19.

People quit after 5 or 6 or 8 or 10 answers because your mind will dry up, but keep pushing, keep squeezing your brain, because you've got the information in there.

The 20th answer often transforms people's lives and takes them from rags to riches.

CHAPTER 5:

EFFECTIVE MARKETING TECHNIQUES

FOR BUSINESS

GREG

I am back with the legendary Brian Tracy, and we've been talking about your business and what your business needs to look like in today's new economy.

In this section we're going to talk about media marketing and PR, and then we're going to get into a little bit of branding. These are some really critical elements in order to take your business from where it is now to where you want it to be going.

You know, Brian, throughout your career you've been a front man in sales and selling your own business and helping other businesses with sales and marketing. I really want to kick this off with maybe some fun stories of some successes you've had in selling and in marketing that really have helped your company and your career take some leaps.

BRIAN

Yes. Well, the critical thing is to find out what is the most pressing need or desire of your customer, and then offer to satisfy that need. We say that a good prospect has a need that is not satisfied and they have this need now. In other words, they're hungry. Sometimes you drive along the highway and they have a great big billboard that'll say, "Hungry?" and they're not looking for someone who's thinking about being hungry; they're looking for someone who's hungry now. Then it'll say, "Turn off at the next exit."

The second thing is that they have a problem unsolved, and the problem is a real concern to them. Third of all they have a goal that has not been achieved, and they want to achieve that goal. Financial independence: the most popular single ad with regard to money is "Lower your taxes."

Everybody wants to reduce your taxes because they consider that money to be literally lost money, and everybody is concerned that they're paying too much and that other people are paying too little. So if we ask a question "Lower your taxes?" it immediately catches people's eye.

The fourth thing is that they have a pain that has not been taken away. The critical thing is immediacy; you're not looking for people to bring in and talk to and convince that they have a need or a problem that your product will solve.

You're looking for people who have it already and are looking for a solution. For example, if you're selling indigestion problems, you say, "Indigestion? Take this!" "Headache? Take that!" "Thirsty? Take one of these!"

In other words, it's very important that you know exactly the most important thing your product or service can do for the customer. Then you find: where are the customers for whom my product or service can do this? Where can they be found?

GREG

I think that's a great place to start. As we build out in this section, we're going to be talking about media marketing and PR. I want to start with media because I think that's the thing that's, for a lot of people, at the front of their mind.

That could be TV; that could be big print; that could be getting in big, major blogs and media. Talk a little bit about how to get into some of those medias, and also: how can that benefit your business?

BRIAN

Okay. Remember, there are 30 million businesses out there right now. Every one of them is fighting desperately to get exposure; you mentioned earlier the importance. The most valuable and most rare commodity in America today is attention, is to get people's attention and hold it.

So therefore, trying to get media exposure is very tough. The average person is exposed to about five thousand commercial messages per day; in newspaper, television, radio, Internet, spam, wherever they go, magazines, there are commercial messages.

The average person has to just blot them all out. To get their attention you've got to be sure your message is getting through. Let me just start off with what I teach to my business owners. There are four parts of marketing strategy that you need to think about.

What is that most valuable work you do in your business? It's thinking clearly. You think clearly with tools. The first tool is called specialization. What is it that you specialize in?

You can specialize in a product or service, you can specialize in a market, a particular type of customer, or you can specialize in a location. A 7-11 specializes in a location. So what do you specialize in? What is your area of specialization?

You never say, "We do everything." A dentist does not do hair and does not paint toenails. A dentist specializes in teeth, and a cosmetic dentist specializes in how pretty your mouth looks.

You've got to be clear about your area of specialty so that a child could tell another child what you do; what it is that you offer. The second key to marketing strategy is differentiation.

Basically, 80% of all marketing is differentiating yourself from your competitors. It's showing your customers that your product or service is better, faster, cheaper, more popular, useable, more convenient; it will make you happier than any other product that's available in the market today in your price category.

A great example is McDonald's. Nobody compares McDonald's with Morton's but in McDonald's price category, which is inexpensive, it focuses on value, quality, price, and cleanliness. In other words, you get good value, you get good quality, you get reasonable prices, and it's clean.

Also, the people are chipper, the facility is nice, so people know they can go to McDonald's and consistently get that quality of experience, and they sell a billion a year in 42,000 outlets. They're the most successful restaurant operation in the history of man on Earth, but at their level.

Therefore, you have to be excellent within your niche. Differentiation; you have to be different. Better, superior, faster, easier, more convenient in three ways in order to compete in today's market. It used to be you had to have one great area of differentiation.

Today it's got to be three, and you have to figure out what those three are. Those are the high ground, and you've got to take the high ground and hold that high ground against your competitors. Don't allow yourself to say, "Oh, we're better in all these areas."

The only time you know is when your customers tell you that you're better. The third area has to do with segmentation, which is: you segment your market and you say, "Where are the customers who most want what I specialize in and who most appreciate and will pay for my area of differentiation?"

You don't advertise Mercedes-Benz in the ghettos and you don't advertise McDonald's in the upper level neighborhoods.

Where are the customers? They say today that all marketing today is segmented marketing; finding your segment.

Then the fourth part is concentration. You advertise, promote, concentrate on the media, the market, the publicity, whatever it is that most reaches the people that you have decided are the very best people who will buy the fastest and pay the most for your product.

So that's strategy, and you have to think it through Specialization, differentiation, segmentation, and concentration: if you miss in any one of those, you go broke, and 80% of of businesses eventually go broke because they don't have answers to those four.

The other thing that is so important is what we call the marketing mix. The marketing mix has seven key parts. The first part is the product or service itself and why it's good and who it's good for.

The second is the price; how much do you charge? You can take a price and charge from $9.95 to $10.05, and your sales will drop 50%. Why? It's because up to $9.95 people will pay it; it's called the no-brainer price.

Once you go over ten dollars, it's "Let me think about it for awhile, and think about it forever." So pricing is really, really important. The third part has to do with promotion. What raise are you going to get the goods out of the woods, get the news to your customers, that the product is available?

I'll give you a very interesting example, a radical theory. A friend of mine opened a first-class restaurant, and rather then spending tens of thousands of dollars advertising this restaurant in a competitive market, what he did is he went down to Yellow Cab in a busy city.

He went down to Yellow Cab and he said, "I'd like to invite your drivers and their wives to come to our restaurant for dinner at no charge, as our guests, next week," just the week prior to opening. Restaurants go through a shakedown phase where they test everything out.

So they gave out these awards to the drivers and their wives, and for the next three or four days the restaurant was full because these were time-limited; full of taxi drivers and their wives. They treated them well and gave them beautiful food and wine and everything was paid for.

And what do you think happened? Every single time a businessperson got into a taxicab and said, "Do you know of a good restaurant to eat at?" they said, "Yeah, this restaurant."

The parking lot was jammed with taxis dropping off businesspeople in twos and foursomes. The restaurant was full for five years because those businesspeople then went out and said, "Geez, I went to a good restaurant last night."

So they put all of their money into free, at the beginning, into the minds and hearts of people who would tell everybody else about it. Great marketing strategy, because that turned out to be cheaper than buying advertising.

The way that you promote your product is really the key. We call this the jelly in the jelly donut. The fourth part has to do with place: where do you sell? There are three others. The three others are packaging: what does your product or service or place of business look like?

You'll find, for example, if you take an Apple product, they are insane about the beauty of the product. As you know, Steve Jobs was insane about making it beautiful, making it thin, making it elegant, so that people held it with pride and handed it to people and people touched it, and they sell them by the tens of millions.

Therefore, how beautiful is your product? It must be as beautiful as or more beautiful than your competitors, or you back to the drawing boards. You should put your packages through this test: ask a kid: "Which one would you pick?"

The kid will always pick the one that looks the most attractive. If you don't pass the kid test, you can go out of business; you can go broke. The sixth part of the marketing mix is people.

The people are the people who actually interact with the customers, and they'd better be really nice, pleasant, polite, cheerful people. Even people behind the counter at McDonald's are trained to be cheerful.

EFFECTIVE MARKETING TECHNIQUES FOR BUSINESS

The last of the seven is positioning, which we'll talk about when we come to branding; how you position yourself in your market and the hearts and minds of your customer is really the critical factor in whether or not you become successful.

GREG

That's really great. I really love all seven of those keys right there in the marketing mix. What I want you to do is I want you to think about how your products and services fit into each of those seven elements.

Go through that in your Action Guide right now, because that's really going to set the tone as you move forward and you create strategies to now go out and market and get the customer. So let's expand on that.

BRIAN

One point: one small change in the marketing mix can transform your business. One change, if it's the right change and the right time, can transform your business; can take you literally from average to extraordinary if it's the right change. So you keep looking as to "How could we improve in one or more of these areas?"

GREG

I like that. Now that we've really thought about these seven areas in the marketing mix, where do we go from there?

BRIAN

You go and you say, "All right, who, where, and what are the media that are already selling to my potential customers?"

I often say to my business audience, "What is the sound that the owl makes in the deep woods?" Everybody thinks about it for a while and then they go, "Whooo? Who?"

Yes. Last year they spent eight billion dollars on market research in the United States alone, asking the question, "Who? Who? Who is my perfect customer? Who is my ideal customer? What is his or her age, occupation, income, educational background, level of family formation, the demographics?

What are his or her psychographics? What are their fears and needs and desires and wants and hopes and aspirations? What moves them emotionally and spiritually and mentally? What's going on in their minds?"

You have to know the answer to the question "Who?" 80% of new products fail each year because they get the 'who' wrong or they don't even think about it. They think, "This is a good product; I think it's a good product. People will buy it."

No; you should be able to tell me, if I were to ask you, "I know a lot of people in this community, Greg. Tell me the kind of people who buy your product or service. Tell me all about them, but don't mention your product or service. I don't want to hear that.

"I don't want to hear the name of your company or your product or service; I just want you to describe the person.

"Who is the person, ideally—what they call the avatar—the person who would be most ideal to buy your product or service immediately and pay a good price for it?"

If you can't do that, then you have to go back to the drawing boards and do it. Most people start off saying, "I'm looking for someone who wants to buy life insurance or who wants to be fitter and healthier and have more energy and everything else."

No; don't talk to me about your product or service because nobody cares what it is; they only care what it does to transform their life in a positive way. So who are these people? Who? Who, and who are they, and then where are they, and why do they buy, and what value do they seek?

Then what are they looking for and what else do they buy, and who are their competitors and why don't they buy, and how could you offset that? The greater clarity you have with regard to your customer, the easier it is to pick media.

Then you find media that are selling effectively to the kind of people that would buy from you. One of the things that we do, you and I do this, and we do this with a lot of other companies, is called joint ventures or strategic alliances; you've heard about other people's money, other people's ideas.

The great breakthrough in small business today is other people's customers, OPC; you find somebody who is already selling to the perfect customer for you and you go to them and say, "Look, let's do a deal.

"Let me sell my products to your customers, non-competing, and I'll share them with you, and then I'll sell your products to my customers. Let's share customers.

"They're all the same type of customers; rather than trying to find new customers, the hardest and most expensive thing in the world today, let's go out and sell to each others' customers."

GREG

Yeah, and make it a win-win for both of us.

BRIAN

Make it win-win; share the revenues.

GREG

Exactly. Now I really want to dig onto something because you hit it on the head when you were talking about people and knowing who your customers are, but also in today's landscape—and this kind of segues into branding—people really do buy from people in today's age.

You mentioned Apple, who we mention a lot; we really can relate to Steve Jobs. We love the products, but we can relate to Steve Jobs. Let's talk about the concept of people buying from people in today's marketplace.

BRIAN

This is very important, but it depends upon your product. People say, and I've taught this for years, is when you are face-to-face with a prospective customer, yes, they buy depending on how they feel about you.

Sometimes I'll ask my audiences, "What percentage of customers' decision-making is emotional? What percentage is logical?" After they say 80/20 or 90/10, I'll say, "No, it's 100% emotional."

When you're dealing directly with another person, the make their decision emotionally and then justify logically. The number one reason that people buy a product or service from a person is because they like the person. I call this relationship selling.

If you're selling your products face-to-face, whether it's in a retail setting or it's direct sales, knocking on doors, talking to people, trade shows, where they're dealing with you, it's how they feel about you. If I like you, and I trust you, and I feel comfortable with you, then I will buy from you, because I will assume that you'll take care of me.

However, if you're selling via Internet—and the Internet is transforming all of marketing—even if you're selling via Internet or via newspapers or direct mail or even radio or newspaper, then it's not the person that's selling; it comes back to the benefit that you're offering.

Once you get people, if you say, for example, "Would you like to save 50% on your taxes this year with a new rule that the IRS has just issued and your accountant doesn't even know about, call this number," that's going to get a lot of people phoning the number.

Then you have to make sure that the person who answers the phone is a really nice person, because the one characteristic of people replying to ads is they are suspicious, because they're afraid that they're going to be hard-sold and up-sold and cross-sold and down-sold.

So make sure the person on the phone is really a nice person and asks really good questions about how they can help this person who called in so the person lets down their guard and relaxes and starts to feel good about who they're talking to. Wherever it's people-to-people selling, then the people doing the selling have got to be genuinely nice people.

GREG

I like that, and some of that's going to go back to the business and the brand and the culture that the business has started. Let's really start to talk about a brand.

So we've gone out, we're going some selling and some marketing, we're getting some data back, we're seeing how people relate to our products and how they buy our products. How does a brand play into that?

I know we were talking earlier: you can't start with a brand; you kind of have to start with your customers and your product and your services, and then you kind of build into that brand.

BRIAN

This is something I know exhaustively; I've taught it for years. Theodore Levitt, who is the dean of Harvard Business School, wrote a book some years ago, a tremendous book. It's called *The Marketing Imagination,* and in that he talked about the most valuable asset that your company has, and it is your reputation with its customers.

Your reputation consists of how you are known to your customers, how your customers think about you when you're not there, how your customers talk about you, how your customers visualize you, how your customers feel when your name is mentioned.

What is the reputation that you have with your customers? That is the most valuable asset you have. Interestingly enough, there's a coffee brand in Hawai'i called Kona Coffee. It's the most popular brand in Hawai'i.

It's interesting; the guys who started this company, entrepreneurs, came up and they decided they wanted to do a leap forward by buying a brand that nobody was taking advantage of.

They stopped selling Kona Coffee 90 years ago, but it was still so famous in Hawai'i they paid $300,000 to buy the name Kona from the ancestors of the people who had built the original coffee company in the last century.

GREG

Wow, that's a strong brand.

BRIAN

Then they took that name and they put it all over everything. Within two years, they're the best-selling coffee in the islands and they sell all over the world because the brand, even though it had not been used for 90 years, was still in the minds and hearts of people; they identified with it.

Black & Decker was sold recently to another major company. They paid $100 million for the company: $10 million for the assets, $90 million dollars for the name Black & Decker because it had such a great name.

So how do you develop this reputation? The question is, you have to ask, "How do we want people to think about us after they've dealt with us? When a person walks away from us, if we were going to interview them, what would we want them to say?

Would we want them to say that our products were excellent, that the service was wonderful, the people were cheerful, the building was efficient? Do we want them to say the packaging was great? What do we want them to say? What impression do we want to leave with them?"

Because that becomes your reputation, and then over time it becomes your brand. First the reputation is what people think clearly; the brand is the instinctive response. For example, lot of research on this: Sony.

When you think of Sony, what do you think? High-quality electronics. Sony can charge 30-40% for the same product that some other company sells using the same components from the same manufacturer.

You put the Sony name on it, the price is worth 30-40%. This brings us to the final point about branding. The best definition I ever saw: "Branding is composed of two elements. Element number one is the promise you make when you ask the customer to buy from you. Element number two is the promise you keep."

So always remember that it's the promise you make and the promise you keep. It's easy to make promises to get people to buy. You can give them discounts, you can deceive them, you can tell them all kinds of wonderful things to get them to buy, but it's the promise you keep that they remember.

When they say, "Yes, you did keep your promise. Yes, it did work. Yes, the food was delicious. Yes, the product was effective. You delivered on your promises and by gum, I'm going to buy again and tell my friends."

GREG

I love it. So now, Brian, as we close out this section I really want to wrap up the sales, the marketing, and the branding, and I want to give everyone listening some actionable steps, because I really want them to take away—as soon as they hit pause—I want them to turn to their team members and have an action plan they can go after.

What can they do right now to really start marketing their business, selling their products, and integrating the brand into that?

BRIAN

Well, you've heard the 80/20 rule. I've said before that marketing and selling is the jelly in the jelly donut. It's the 80% that accounts for everything. Everything else you do in the business is the bread part of the jelly donut.

If you are serious about your business, then you think about marketing which is attracting people who are interested, who have a need, a want, a desire, and selling, which is persuading them to buy from you rather than someone else who can satisfy the same need.

Marketing is attracting qualified prospects; selling is converting them. Every company—95% of companies—can be better at this. If you're not really good at selling, get good at selling.

Listen to the best audio programs, take the courses, read the books; your ability to convert interested prospects into customers determines your entire life. Here's the wonderful thing: all marketing skills are learnable.

All sales skills are learnable. All business skills are learnable. You can learn every skill you need to learn in order to achieve any business goal you can set for yourself, but you've got to become deadly serious about marketing and attracting new people.

Forget all the little nonsense that you do during the course of the day. There's a beautiful line that says, "Social networking is social not working."; this is not a way of generating customers, it's a way of having communications with people. If you develop a customer after ten years, God bless you.

Your job is to get out there and talk to customers; talk to them on the Internet, talk to them on the phone, talk to them person-to-person, but your job is to be literally obsessed with contacting, communication, and talking to customers, explaining to them why they will be so much better off than they are now if they buy your product or service, and you must do this from dawn to dusk.

Do your paperwork before 8:00 in the morning and after 6:00 at night, and between eight and six do nothing but think about attracting and converting people into buying what you sell.

GREG

That's really, really powerful information that you just shared. Go back, and if you need to learn some selling skills, go learn it. Find the master in sales that you can learn from; find the master in marketing, find the master in business, and really improve those areas in your business.

Go back into Brian's seven areas of the marketing mix and look at all those, and again, look at how you can insert your products and services into that marketing mix and really get the results that you want out of your business.

In the next part of this program, we're going to come back and we're going to talk about really recession-proofing your business and how you can build a business that's not going to last just through the next year and get through payroll, but how it can last and stand the test of time. So go through your Action Guide, and we will see you again in the next section.

SUMMARY

THE 4 KEYS TO MARKETING STRATEGY

1. SPECIALIZATION

You can specialize in a product or service, you can specialize in a market, a particular type of customer, or you can specialize in a location. What is your area of specialization? Never say, "We do everything."

2. DIFFERENTIATION

Pick 3 ways in which you are better, superior, faster, or easier than your competitors. Don't allow yourself to say you are better than your competitors in all areas. Focus your service and your marketing on the key differentiators.

3. SEGMENTATION

Where are the customers who most want what I specialize in and will pay for my area of differentiation? Don't advertise Mercedes-Benz in the ghettos and don't advertise McDonald's in expensive neighborhoods. Find your segment and stick to it.

4. CONCENTRATION

Concentrate on the media, the market, the publicity, whatever it is that most reaches the people that you have decided are the very best people for your product. Don't get distracted, concentrate on doing more and going deeper within your focus.

THE 80/20 RULE

Marketing and selling are the 80% that matters. Marketing is attracting qualified prospects; selling is converting them. Everything else in business is secondary to this 80%.

CHAPTER 6:

BUILDING AN EVERLASTING BUSINESS

GREG

Hi, this is Greg Rollett and welcome back to the series on building a thriving business in today's economy. Today we've been joined by the legendary Brian Tracy.

Brian's been sharing some of his best secrets to creating a business that is successful in using marketing, media, PR, and branding to really get your business in the position it needs to be in order to be more successful. Here in this section we're going to be talking about recession-proofing your business and building a business that has a lasting legacy.

I really wanted to start by talking about your business, because your business has been able to survive through multiple presidents and different economic situations and different price points for your products. How do you think you've been able to really survive and change and continue to grow through all these different circumstances?

BRIAN

You hear a lot about innovation today; innovation and creativity. Basically, what it means is you're constantly looking for faster, newer, better, easier, cheaper, more convenient ways to generate revenues.

The key to the success of your business is cash flow. If you have positive cash flow, you survive. If you have negative cash flow for any period of time, you die.

As Jack Welch, the CEO of General Electric, once said, if there's anything that you would do to save your business if worse came to worst, don't wait; do it now.

Throw everything off the ship to keep the ship afloat. Lay people off, fire people, cut back, but remember this: there's a great piece of work called *Profit From the Core*, and I teach it all over the place.

Basically what it says it that a business starts off with a core product or service that the business owner and people are good at producing and it's profitable, and that's where every business starts, whether it's cookies or donuts or something else.

Then they begin to expand, and as they expand, they tend to expand into areas that they hope will be really profitable, but often are not as profitable as the core business.

Then they expand into other areas, and this s the natural tendency of companies, to keep expanding into areas that are not as profitable as the core business, and if they're not careful, what they do is they take their eye off the ball and their competitors go in and grab the core business.

So when the market starts to turn down, what you have to do is you have to pull back in like an army camp; pull your soldiers back in to defend the core. You have to start discontinuing all low-profit, no-profit activities and do it quickly.

Get your ego out of the way; we're talking about survival here. Get your ego out of the way and get back to those products and services. As they say, "Dance with the one what brought you."

Get back to the products and services that were the ones you established your business on, and make sure that your business is profitable. Cash flow, positive cash flow, is everything, and you as the business owner are 100% responsible for the survival of your business.

You must make any decisions, any hard decisions, any cold decisions, but you've got to assure survival, and that means you've got to have cash. You've got to pay down debt; you've got to insist on payment from your customers; you've got to negotiate better and tougher terms; you've got to do everything to assure survival.

If you have that mindset, then the next thing you do is say, "What other products or services could we introduce to the market that are an extension, a logical extension, of our key skills, our core competencies, what we do really well?"

Like a McDonald's can bring out a salad or a McRib or something else; they're not starting a donut business across the street, they're doing a natural and logical brand extension or product/service extension from what they're already good at.

As a matter of fact, there's a little book that's called *Small Bets*, and what it says is you don't have to bet your whole company; experiment with one small new product and see how the market responds. The rule is: the only test is a market test. The only true test is a customer test.

By the way, a great way we teach this, to test a product or service, is if you have a good idea, call one of your customers and say, "Look, I've got a good idea for this product or service. What do you think?" Customers are amazing; they will tell you like that, exactly if it's a good idea.

Then you say, "How much would you pay for this? I'd probably have to charge this kind of money in order to bring it to the market. How much would you pay?" They'll say, "That's a reasonable price," or "No, I wouldn't pay that much," or "I'd pay even more than that if it will actually do what you say it will do."

You talk to ten customers and they will show you how to recession-proof your business. The other thing is the hardest thing to do is to get a new customer. The easiest thing to do is to take a satisfied customer and sell them more stuff.

The easiest thing beyond that is to get referrals from satisfied customers. A good friend of mine was called by a person whose business was going through a recession and said, "What can I do? No matter how much I advertise, I can't seem to attract more business," which is quite common.

He said, "Go back to every customer you've had for the last two or three years and tell them, 'Thank you for your business; would you like to buy some more?'" The guy went back and did that; within 60 days he increased his sales 40%; went from being in the red to being in the black.

He said he could not believe how much extra business there was just by asking his happy customers to buy some more. Then he said, "Would you happen to know anybody else who might be interested in what we sell?" and he started to get a river of referrals and new business.

He reduced his advertising and promotion, he put all of his focus and time and telephone calls and personal visits on his existing good customers, and they saved his life.

That's one of the most wonderful things you can do, is of course get new businesses with new products and services, but take fabulous care of your existing customers and get them to buy more.

GREG

That's a great, great strategy because there's really this money just sitting there.

BRIAN

Yes, because they already know you. They already like you; they already trust you; they've already given you money; they've already enjoyed your product or service. Say, "Hey, come on down and do it again!"

GREG

Something that I want to talk about, especially in today's economy and today's age, is attention. We sort of talked a little bit about this in marketing, that our attention spans are shorter, we have sites like YouTube that instead of watching a 30-minute TV show, we're watching a 3-minute video clip.

You have technology that's increasing and just the amount of content that's needed to put out there. Just yourself, you're doing blog posts; you're doing videos; you're doing speaking; you're writing books. There's just a lot that goes into keeping a customer's attention. Can you talk about how that affects business today?

BRIAN

You have to realize that 99% of the time people think about themselves; that a person is more concerned about a split fingernail that they have that they want to get repaired than if 100,000 people are washed out into the ocean in a flood in Bangladesh.

So therefore, if you want to hold people's attention, you have to keep answering the question "What's in it for me?" What's in it for me? What's in it for me? If you want to get people's you have to constantly be addressing what it is that they want and what they need and what they care about.

It's interesting; they will show photographs to men or women to find out what causes pupil dilation, because pupil dilation is the very best indicator of interest. When a person sees something of interest, their pupils dilate.

You know what they find that causes men's pupils to dilate the fastest? Of course, it's pictures of attractive women. What causes women's pupils to dilate is pictures of babies. It's automatic; you show those pictures.

I only tell you that example because your description of your product or service has got to cause pupil dilation. It's got to cause people to pay attention, jerk awake, because it's connecting with something that they really want and need and care about; a pain that they have or a goal they want to achieve.

If you can offer that, then you'll get their attention, and if you keep offering that, like for example we used to say that if you can get people to say 'yes' six times in a sales presentation, then they'll buy your product.

Six 'yeses' and they become like a little dog. So I would be selling investments, and I say, "Would you like to see an investment that'll pay you a tremendous rate of return with no risk?" "Absolutely."

"Would you like to become financially independent?" "Yes." "Would you like to have investment that is better than what you have already?" These are the same questions. "Yes."

"Would you like to have an investment that you can afford us to manage for you so it assures high returns?" "Yes." "Would you want an investment that will enable you to sleep well at night because you don't have to worry about it?" "Yes."

It's the same question asked six different times; it's six different benefits of making a good investment. If the person says yes, by the time they've said yes the sixth time, their buying temperature is buying and they want to use your product or service.

Really good advertising and promotion keeps addressing the fundamental need; with regard to money, it's for security and growth. That's what people want. They keep repeating, "Would you like more security? More growth? More growth? More security?" Growth and security; security and growth.

The other person is saying "Yes, yes, yes, yes," and it's the same thing with beautiful foods and lovely restaurants and beautiful decor and lovely lighting and wonderful service and beautiful dishware and fabulous food; it's all a description of the restaurant.

As long as you're describing what the customer wants and needs and is willing to pay for emotionally as well as logically, you'll have their total attention.

GREG

I like that a lot. Attention is very, very important. As we talk about a business that we want to last, there are things that we're going to have to do on a day-to-day basis in order for out business to be here one year, five years, ten years, twenty years down the road.

We've talked about goals, we've talked about marketing, we've talked about sales, but what are some things that business owners really need to think about on a day-to-day basis that are going to impact them years down the road and make sure they're profitable?

BRIAN

Here's an important point: life, as you say, is the study of attention. Therefore, what business owners pay attention to largely determines the direction of their business. It's like the guidance system in the guided missile.

If business owners pay attention to social media, then the company will go nowhere. If business owners are obsessed with selling, obsessed with top line, top line, top line- good business owners are asking every hour: "How much did we sell?"

Every day: "What were our sales today?" Every week: "How much cash do we have in the bank?" Every month: "What were our sales and profitability?"

Whatever the business owner pays attention to the most, that's the direction the whole company goes in. Everybody follows the lead of the business owner, so therefore if you want to build a long-term business, one of the things that we talk about is you've got to get control of your debt.

You've got to have no debt or low debt, and the only debt you have should be debt that is serviceable by your positive cash flow. The businesses that succeed the most are the ones that have cash.

Did you know that Apple is sitting on $50 billion in cash today? That Microsoft is sitting on $46 billion in cash? These are the most successful companies in the world; they have choices.

They can plan for the future; they can invest in new products and services because they have cash in the bank. So you as the business owner: pay attention to the cash.

How much cash? Pay attention to the sales; how much revenue? Pay attention to the receivables. Pay attention to the payables.

It's the most important thing you can do because you build a long-term business by building a really strong short-term business. You build your business day-by-day, week-by-week, month-by-month; it'll build itself year-by-year.

GREG

I love it; I think that's great information to leave you guys on today as we wrap up this third and final section. What I encourage you to do is really go back and listen to everything that Brian has shared with you and really start to apply it to your business.

It's only those that take action that get results, and that's a really, really strong part of this course. Brian's given you some actionable tips, strategies, and things that you can turn around and implement right now in your business, day to day. Get that cash flow going and you're going to see a very successful business in the future. Brian, I want to thank you for joining us today.

BRIAN

Thank you, Greg.

GREG

Again, I encourage you guys to take action, and we look forward to seeing your successful businesses for years to come.

SUMMARY

CASH FLOW IS KING

The key to the success of your business is cash flow. If you have positive cash flow, you survive. If you have negative cash flow for any period of time, you die.

DON'T FORGET YOUR EXISTING CUSTOMERS

Go back to every customer you've had for the last two or three years and tell them, 'Thank you for your business; would you like to buy some more?" You can generate cash flow quickly without the outlay of advertising.

GET THE ATTENTION OF PROSPECTS

Attention is very scarce in this day of technology and media overload. If you want to grab people's attention, you have to keep answering the question "What's in it for me?" What's in it for me? What's in it for me?" Constantly address what it is that they want, what they need, and what they care about.

FOCUS YOUR OWN ATTENTION

What business owners pay attention to largely determines the direction of their business. It's like the guidance system in the guided missile. Be obsessed with your sales, review sales numbers every day. Be obsessed with controlling debt and building up cash.

ABOUT THE AUTHORS

ALEX GOLDSTEIN is a top producing real estate agent based in Arizona. He represents high net worth families on luxury home purchases and sales, and also represents investors seeking competitive returns on investment properties.

In addition to representing clients in real estate transactions, Alex has been a principal in over $50 million of real estate transactions including land, office, and residential properties. Alex's investment background started early in his career as a bond trader, where he managed over $500 million for the world's largest insurance broker, Aon Corporation. He left Aon to start one of the first ecommerce sites in the life insurance industry, one which became profitable and thrived through the dot com bust of the early 2000's and still exists today.

Alex is an honors graduate of Northwestern University, and was also a visiting scholar at Oxford University. He is passionate about food and wine, having served on the boards of the International Wine & Food Society and the Confrérie des Chevaliers du Tastevin.

BRIAN TRACY is Chairman and CEO of Brian Tracy International, a company specializing in the training and development of individuals and organizations. Brian's goal is to help you achieve your personal and business goals faster and easier than you ever imagined.

Brian Tracy has consulted for more than 1,000 companies and addressed more than 5,000,000 people in 5,000 talks and seminars throughout the US, Canada and 55 other countries worldwide. As a Keynote speaker and seminar leader, he addresses more than 250,000 people each year.

He has studied, researched, written and spoken for 30 years in the fields of economics, history, business, philosophy and psychology. He is the top selling author of over 45 books that have been translated into dozens of languages.

He has written and produced more than 300 audio and video learning programs, including the worldwide, best-selling Psychology of Achievement, which has been translated into more than 20 languages.

He has traveled and worked in over 80 countries on six continents, and speaks four languages. Brian is happily married and has four children. He is active in community and national affairs, and is the President of three companies headquartered in Solana Beach, California.

FREE SPECIAL OFFER FOR READERS

The information in this book is useless if you don't apply it. Please take immediate action to benefit you and your family in real estate, business, and financial decisions.

To help, we are making available to all readers an Action Guide that provides step-by-step instructions to apply the techniques in this book. For this free resource, please visit:

www.HomeIncBook.com/SecretBonus

www.ingramcontent.com/pod-product-compliance
Lightning Source LLC
Chambersburg PA
CBHW021547200526
45163CB00016B/2715

* 9 7 8 1 4 9 2 8 1 2 7 3 9 *